Everyday Asian

Also by Patricia Yeo (and Julia Moskin)

Cooking from A to Z

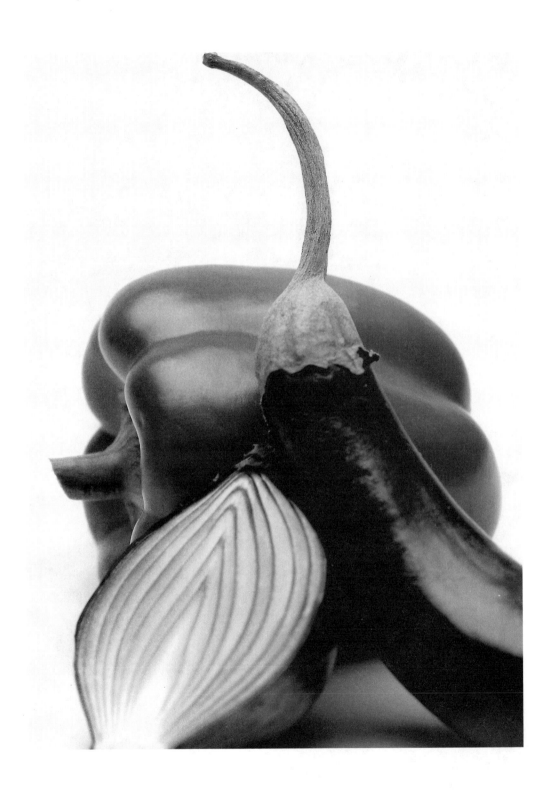

Everyday Asian

Asian Flavors + Simple Techniques = 120 Mouthwatering Recipes

Patricia Yeo and Tom Steele

Photographs by Alex Martinez

St. Martin's Press ✻ New York

www.stmartins.com

Book design by rlf design

LIBRARY OF CONGRESS CATALOGING-IN-PUBLICATION DATA

Yeo, Patricia.
    Everyday Asian : Asian flavors + simple techniques = 120 mouthwatering recipes / Patricia Yeo and Tom Steele.
        p. cm.
    ISBN 0-312-29028-4
    EAN 978-0-312-29028-3
    1. Cookery, Asian. I. Steele, Tom, 1952 March 30–. II. Title.

TX724.5.A1Y45 2005
641.595—dc22

2005044232

First Edition: October 2005

10   9   8   7   6   5   4   3   2   1

Contents

Acknowledgments

Patricia Yeo:

I want to extend my deepest thanks to all my kitchen staff at Sapa. You have kept me sane when I should really have gone mad, especially Gavin Portsmouth, Damien Brassel, Josh Rubin, and Peter Endriss.

Special thanks also to Ruben, JD, Jesse, and Brian for their endless support in my every endeavor.

To Scott Replogle, heartfelt thanks for being there and being so special.

Superagent Stacey Glick at Dystel and Goderich Literary Management has the perspicacity and resourcefulness of ten agents.

Elizabeth Beier at St. Martin's is a dream editor, with an eagle eye for detail and a soaring heart—and appetite!

As always, I'm grateful for the love and support of my sister Jackie, my brother-in-law John, my mother, and my Fourth Auntie.

Tom Steele:

I want to single out several people whose direct contributions to my cooking and food writing are inestimable.

My mother, a terrific cook, encouraged me from the time I was about four years old to explore cooking with her and on my own. We trade recipes to this very day. My sisters, Rusty and Marcia, were certainly along for the ride as I learned to cook, and they have never stopped believing in me.

Chuck Ortleb was the first to nudge me in the direction of food writing by having me review restaurants for two of his publications, which I also edited, *New York Native*

Acknowledgments

x

and *Theater Week*. He has inspired me in countless other ways as well.

The infinitely talented Rebecca Bent gave me my first real break in the cookbook world by choosing me to pull together her first cookbook, *Burgers*. Her faith in me and her enduring friendship are beyond inspiring. She makes everything shine.

Over the years, Tom Miller has given me more moral support than he could possibly realize, and so have marvelous Jim Pellegrinon and Neenyah Ostrom. We've all cooked for one another, too, and quite well.

Rodger Parsons, Glenn Wein, and Adam Kowit have all been right by my side when I needed encouragement or advice—and when I've needed very hungry and knowledgeable restaurant reviewing partners.

Brendan Lemon has always been just princely, and has given me such wonderful opportunities and such joy.

Raymond Luczak, the deeply gifted man I've cooked for every night I've been home for fifteen years, has shaped my cooking much more than he knows.

Our agent Stacey Glick at Dystel and Goderich Literary Management is absolutely mercurial, possessing true vision and compassion.

Our marvelous editor, Elizabeth Beier, is among the sharpest and most delightful people I've ever met in publishing. And best of all, we quickly became good friends.

Patricia Yeo has been my favorite collaborator of all time: endlessly resourceful, faster than a roadrunner, generous to the marrow—and one of the greatest chefs in America.

Introduction

Cooking with Five Senses

Just as it has been my duty in my Manhattan restaurants to entice and delight you with scrumptious dishes you probably won't find anywhere else, I feel that it is my obligation with this book to make your own cooking sing in different keys.

My cooking is idiosyncratic; yours should be, too. My goal is to free you from the shackles of recipes even as I provide them as blueprints. Customize your cooking! You can—and should—make any recipe your own by imparting your own personal sense of flavors and textures. Recipes are not meant to be straitjackets. Rather, they are an outline for each cook to fill in with variable ingredients and even cooking methods. Recipes are evolving, living things that should grow with you as your confidence and cooking skills increase.

I remember attending a round-table discussion about culinary trends in America in general and in New York City in particular. The general conclusion we came to was that the notion of comfort food in this country has expanded from mashed potatoes, macaroni and cheese, pork chops, and applesauce to include dishes like pad thai, pasta alla carbonara, sushi, and couscous. That's the way I feel about the recipes and ingredients in this book. Ingredients like fish sauce, fermented black beans, and lemongrass are no longer exotic; they have become staples in lots of pantries throughout the country.

I am always amazed by the similarities between ingredients from region to region. Fish sauce, after all, is the anchovy of Southeast Asia, fermented black beans taste remarkably like Moroccan oil-cured olives, and lemongrass can be substituted for lemon balm or lemon verbena.

This may sound strange coming from someone writing a cookbook, but I truly believe that we are too dogmatic and rigid when it comes to recipes. I have tried hard to give the reader as many options and alternatives as possible in the hope that they will see that recipes are not meant to be followed to a T. Food is not meant to be taken so seriously: It's about comfort, family, and warmth, not dogma. If you prefer the flavor of anchovies to the flavor of fish sauce, then by all means use it in your pad thai. If you prefer lemongrass to lemon balm or lemon verbena, then use it in your panna cotta. Play with ingredients, substitute liberally, and if you particularly like something, then use it. The same applies to recipes: They should be used as road maps, with the certain knowledge that there are many alternate routes to reach the final destination.

I want to show the home cook how to use all five senses when cooking. Look at the quality of a piece of cod, for instance; listen to it sizzle as it hits the hot buttered skillet, smell it as it caramelizes in the pan, touch it with the tips of your fingers to gauge its doneness, and finally, taste it. That's how we should all cook. Cooking is not a science; you cannot follow every

recipe to the letter. For instance, during the summer, a piece of cod is a lot less dense than it is in the middle of winter, and, therefore, the cooking time is going to be different. I want to help the home cook to start thinking about cooking in these terms.

The recipes that I give my restaurant cooks consist simply of a list of ingredients, with no quantities or cooking techniques. I realize that this is not realistic in a cookbook, but I want the home cook to know that the quantity of ingredients and the amount of time it takes to cook a piece of fish, for instance, are somewhat arbitrary factors. I cannot know how hot your burners get, or calculate the thickness of the bottoms of your pots and pans—still more factors that affect cooking times and the outcome of the finished dish. Keeping this in mind, I would like to repeat: Use my recipes as guidelines. Have fun and be creative.

Chefs try to make each dish unique. We weave flavors together: a little maple syrup and honey to tame the spice of a blistering curry; bits of crispy, salty bacon to add interest to roasted cauliflower—that's what makes my dishes different from yours. The ability and confidence to pair flavors comes naturally to some of us, while in others it is something learned by remembering something we ate or read about. I will try to give you a quick road map to pairing flavors by including lists of serving ideas to vary each recipe, as well as helpful hints about various ingredients.

In short, I want the home cook to start thinking more like a chef, and to begin adapting and renovating classic recipes to reflect personal tastes and preferences.

We all lead busy lives, and cooking our daily meals should be a simple, straightforward, and enjoyable activity. Most of the recipes in this book will require as little equipment as possible. One pot, one mixing bowl, and a cutting board are all you will need for many of these dishes. If a recipe calls for chicken or beef stock, I don't expect you to make your own. There are a great many wonderful ready-made food products out there, so use store-bought if you don't have the time. But I will also include some more involved dishes for weekend meals and special occasions.

Above all, I want to encourage home cooks to include Asian dishes as part of their everyday menus. With this book, I've tried to make doing that as easy as possible without "dumbing down" the techniques (many of which are simple to begin with) or sacrificing the marvelous textures and flavors of these cuisines.

So remember: Bring all five senses—and a sense of playfulness—to the kitchen with you, and you will always emerge with quite special food for yourself, your family, and your friends.

Salads

Salads are a large part of my diet. I love big composed salads that can be served as an entrée for lunch or as a light supper when it's too hot to *think* about cooking. In *Cooking from A to Z*, I tried to bring new flavors to classic American favorites. In this book, I wanted to introduce some more unusual salads, like *fattoush* and *laabs*, using flavors and ingredients that are familiar to everyone.

Grilled Shrimp and Indian Bread Salad

This bread salad is an Indian spin on Tuscan bread salad; instead of using pieces of stale peasant bread, I use pieces of naan or roti. Actually, it's more like a *fattoush*, which is the Middle Eastern version made with toasted stale pita bread. Note that if you use curry oil, it needs to steep for an hour.

Makes 4 light main course servings

1 tomato, diced

1 small red onion, finely diced

½ cup diced celery

½ cup diced cucumber

Salt and freshly ground black pepper to taste

Juice of 1 lemon

½ cup diced grilled zucchini

½ cup diced roasted peppers (see Options below)

½ cup pieces blanched green beans (cut into 1-inch pieces)

4 pieces naan or roti, torn into bite-sized pieces (see Options below)

½ cup cilantro leaves

½ cup flat parsley leaves

5 large Boston lettuce leaves, torn into bite-sized pieces

½ cup curry oil (see Options below)

20 grilled shrimp (see Options below)

In a large bowl, combine the tomato, onion, celery, and cucumber. Toss lightly with a little salt, pepper, and lemon juice; allow to sit for up to a half hour. The salt will draw out the juices from the vegetables. Add the other vegetables and naan. Toss well, allowing the vegetable juices to soak into the bread. Just before serving, toss with herbs, lettuce, and curry oil. Garnish with grilled shrimp, five per serving.

Options

➢ I like using a mixture of roasted red peppers and poblano peppers because I like the sharpness of poblanos.

➢ To make the curry oil, mix two tablespoons of curry powder with enough water to make a paste. Slowly stir in ½ cup canola or other mild oil. Let the mixture stand for an hour, strain it, and it's ready to use. Store the oil, covered tightly, in the refrigerator if you're not using it immediately.

➢ If you don't have roti or naan, use pita or whatever bread you have lying around. Stale bread is preferable. No stale bread? Make some: Simply tear up pieces of bread, spread them on a cookie sheet, and dry them out in a low oven (150 degrees or just with the pilot) for half an hour.

➢ Substitute slices of cool roast lamb or roast chicken for the grilled shrimp.

Green Mango Salad

Green mango has a flavor more like a vegetable than a fruit. It is crisp, slightly tart, and tastes like a cross between a green apple and a cucumber. In fact, if you are unable to find green mangoes in your market, just substitute a mixture of green apples and cucumber. In Thailand toasted ground rice is added to green mango salads, giving it additional flavor and a textural element. Ground rice is raw rice that is toasted until it is golden then ground in a spice grinder—easy enough to do yourself.

Makes 4 servings

1 cup julienned green mango

¼ cup julienned carrot

¼ cup julienned jicama

¼ cup julienned red pepper

2 tablespoons Lemongrass Caramel Vinaigrette (recipe follows)

Juice of 1 lime

¼ cup mint leaves

¼ cup cilantro leaves

¼ cup toasted chopped peanuts (optional)

Toasted ground rice (optional; see Option below)

Toss all the julienned vegetables with the vinaigrette and lime juice. Allow to macerate for up to a half hour. Just before serving, toss in the mint and cilantro. If you like, add the toasted peanuts at this point and toss well.

Option

➢ If you want to add toasted ground rice, add it with the peanuts and herbs at the last moment.

Lemongrass Caramel Vinaigrette
Makes about 1 cup

**1 stalk lemongrass, tough top and
bottom removed and discarded,
thinly sliced**

2 cloves garlic, peeled

**2 nickel-sized slices ginger,
unpeeled**

1 shallot, coarsely chopped

**1 jalapeño pepper, stemmed and
coarsely chopped**

1 teaspoon red pepper flakes

½ cup sugar

¼ cup Thai fish sauce

Juice of 2 limes

1½ teaspoons toasted sesame oil

About ½ cup canola oil

Place the lemongrass, garlic, and ginger in the workbowl of a food processor. Add the shallot, jalapeño, and pepper flakes, and process until the mixture is finely ground. Set aside.

Pour the sugar into a medium-sized heavy saucepan and set it over medium-high heat. Cook, stirring with a wooden spoon to break up any lumps, until the sugar melts and turns amber, about 5 minutes. Add the lemongrass mixture and cook for 1 minute, stirring constantly. (The mixture will seize up at first, but then smooth out.) Carefully add the fish sauce and simmer, stirring, for 30 seconds. Remove from the heat and let cool to room temperature. When cooled, whisk in the lime juice, sesame oil, and canola oil to taste. Use at once or refrigerate, covered, for up to 1 week.

Chicken Waldorf Salad

This salad is great for lunch or to bring along for a potluck dinner. It's a substantial change from the ubiquitous Caesar salad with grilled chicken. I like using different varieties of apples in the salad, some Granny Smith for tartness, Fuji for the texture and sweetness, and perhaps an apple with a softer texture, like Golden Delicious. If you don't want to make your own mayonnaise just use your favorite store-bought.

Makes 4 servings

2 cups diced roasted chicken (see Options below)
2 cups peeled and diced apples (see Options below)
1 cup large-diced celery
½ cup toasted walnuts
Juice of 1 lemon
1 cup mayonnaise
Salt and freshly ground black pepper to taste
4 large Boston lettuce leaves

Mix everything together except the salt, pepper, and lettuce. Taste and season well with salt and pepper. Serve the salad in the lettuce leaves.

Options

➢ Use other roasted meats, or if you are vegetarian, tempeh works well, too.

➢ Add some halved grapes to the salad; just reduce the amount of apples.

Chinese Chicken Salad with Pickled Vegetables

This is one of my mother's recipes. It's simple and straightforward, and can be made in advance, which makes it a great dish to take to family gatherings. Pickled vegetables are available at most Asian markets, or see Ingredient Sources, page 199.

Makes 4 servings

4 poached boneless skinless chicken breasts

½ cup each pickled carrots, daikon radish (page 179), and red onion (available in most Asian markets)

½ cup each finely julienned napa cabbage

½ cup peeled and julienned cucumber

1 cup mayonnaise

½ cup pickled ginger

½ cup toasted sesame seeds

Shred the chicken, and toss with the remaining ingredients.

Salads

Malaysian Spicy Fruit Salad

There is a wonderful Malaysian salad called *rojak*, often sold as street food. It is spicy, sweet, and tart, all at the same time. My Fourth Auntie (who is my favorite aunt) loves it and I always think of her when I make this side dish, especially since she now lives in New Zealand where it is nearly impossible to get green mango, shrimp paste, and many of the other ingredients needed for this salad. Luckily, in almost any large city in America, you can find these ingredients pretty easily. Ketchup or *kecap manis* is a sweet, thick soy sauce common in Southeast Asia, rather like hoisin sauce. It's available in many Asian specialty stores or grocery stores.

Makes 4 to 6 servings

2 tablespoons shrimp paste
   (optional; see Options below)

1 tablespoon *kecap manis*

1 teaspoon sugar

Juice of 2 limes

1 green mango, cut into bite-sized
   pieces (see Options below)

1 cup bite-sized chunks pineapple

1 cup bite-sized pieces jicama

1 cup blanched water spinach (see
   Options below)

1 cup bite-sized chunks firm tofu
   (see Note below)

¼ cup toasted peanuts

Toss all the ingredients except the peanuts together in a large bowl. Sprinkle the top of the salad with the peanuts and serve at room temperature.

Note: I usually toss all the ingredients together, then fold in the tofu as it sometimes falls apart and I like my tofu in large pieces. If you don't mind your tofu a little beaten up, then mix it all up together.

Options

➢ If you cannot find shrimp paste
in your nearest Chinese market,
try using dried shrimp (which
can more easily be found in
Asian as well as Mexican markets). Pan-fry the dried shrimp
in a little oil until crisp, then
roughly chop it up and toss it
into the salad. The flavor of the
dried shrimp can be a little
strong, so use it judiciously.

➢ You can substitute a tart green
apple like Granny Smith.

➢ You can substitute blanched asparagus, cut into 1-inch lengths.

Grilled Asparagus Salad with Poached Egg and Shaved Parmesan

After a long winter of cold, snow, and root vegetables, I always look forward to the first asparagus in the spring. I like to cook tender pencil asparagus on the grill. There is no need to blanch it first.

Makes 4 servings

4 large eggs

¼ cup white vinegar

1½ quarts water

40 stalks pencil asparagus (see Options below)

½ cup extra-virgin olive oil

Salt and freshly ground black pepper to taste

2 lemons, preferably Meyer lemons, juiced

1 shallot, finely diced

4 pieces grilled sourdough bread, ½-inch thick

1 cup (or more) freshly shaved Parmigiano-Reggiano cheese

Add vinegar and water to a large saucepan and bring to a simmer.

Break the eggs into the simmering vinegared water and poach for 4 minutes. Remove the eggs from the water with a slotted spoon, and keep them warm.

Toss the asparagus in ¼ cup of the oil, mixed with the salt and pepper, and grill for 3 minutes (I like the asparagus to char a little). Transfer to a bowl, add the lemon juice, shallot, and the remaining olive oil. Toss well. Serve the asparagus on grilled bread with the poached eggs and lots of shaved Parmesan.

Options

➤ Serve the asparagus with really soft scrambled eggs on grilled bread for breakfast. If you feel like treating yourself, add a slice or two of cured salmon.

➤ When you trim the woody ends off the asparagus, don't discard them. I usually save mine to toss into stock. Asparagus-flavored stock is especially great for a vegetarian risotto or asparagus soup. Store the asparagus stems tightly wrapped in the freezer until you're ready to make stock. They'll keep there for up to 8 months.

➤ Try roasting your asparagus to concentrate the flavors, or stir-fry it. Blanching is my least favorite way to cook asparagus because too much of the flavor leaches out into the blanching liquid.

Salads

Smoked Mussels and Potato Salad with Mustard Seeds

I am very fond of smoked fish and shellfish, probably because growing up in England, kippers and smoked oysters were considered a treat. I remember toasting bread over an open fire, then buttering and eating it with smoked oysters my first winter at school. I have been trying to recapture that taste ever since. This smoked mussel salad is a grown-up and more subtle version of that flavor. The mussels are steamed and smoked at the same time. They are sweet and delicate, a perfect foil for the nuttiness of the mustard seeds and the acidity of the lemons.

Makes 4 servings

2 tablespoons gold mustard seeds

2 tablespoons black mustard seeds

¼ cup mayonnaise

4 tablespoons capers, rinsed and chopped

2 tablespoons Dijon mustard

Juice and grated zest of 1 lemon

10 small Yukon gold potatoes, boiled until just tender and sliced

¾ cup Lapsang Souchong tea

¼ cup dark brown sugar

2 tablespoons smashed star anise

40 mussels, scrubbed, "beards" removed, and dried (see Options below)

1 bunch watercress sprigs for garnish

Toast the mustard seeds in a dry pan over medium heat until they start to pop, about 5 minutes. Transfer the seeds into a mixing bowl with the mayonnaise, capers, mustard, and juice and zest of lemon. Mix.

Add the sliced Yukon gold potatoes while they're still warm, to absorb the flavors of the mayonnaise mixture.

Line the bottom of a heavy pot with a tight-fitting lid with two layers of aluminum foil. Spread the tea, brown sugar, and star anise over the foil. Place the mussels directly on the mixture and turn the heat to high. Once the mixture starts to smoke, after about 3 minutes, put the lid on, and reduce the heat to medium. Cook for another 5 to 8 minutes, until all the mussels have opened. Remove the mussels (discarding any that haven't opened), shuck them, and reserve.

Just before serving, toss the mussels and any juices that have collected with the potato mixture. Serve with sprigs of watercress as a garnish.

Options

➢ Try using smoked fish. An oily fish like bluefish is really deli-cious. You can use store-bought smoked fish, but it's easy to smoke your own. Just substitute fish for the mussels in the recipe.

➢ Smoked mussels or fish is deli-cious tossed with pasta and lots of lemon juice, mustard, and herbs for a quick salad.

➢ Or make a smoky fish mousse by pureeing smoked fish with a little cream cheese, lemon juice, and scallions as a spread for toasted bagels.

Salmon Sashimi Salad

This dish is a cross between sashimi and a salad. It makes a perfect summer lunch because the only cooking involved is steaming the sushi rice—everything else is chilled. Sushi rice is best eaten the day it is cooked. Refrigerated, it becomes hard, although I've been told that if you warm it in a microwave oven, it will soften again.

Makes 4 servings

1 cup diced avocado

½ cup diced cucumber

¼ cup Pickled Carrots (available in most Asian markets)

1 cup cooked sushi rice

4 ounces sushi-grade salmon, cut into ¼-inch slices (see Options below)

¼ cup grated daikon radish

2 tablespoons *sambal* (Indonesian spice blend, available in most Asian markets)

2 scallions, trimmed and sliced lengthwise into ribbons

Soy sauce and wasabi for dipping

Toss the avocado, cucumber, and carrots together in a medium bowl. Divide the rice among four serving bowls. Divide the salmon slices evenly among the bowls, draping them over the rice. Mix the grated daikon and *sambal* together, scatter a small spoonful of the mixture over each portion, and garnish with the scallion ribbons. Serve with the soy sauce and wasabi.

Options

➢ Instead of salmon, use tuna, fluke, or your favorite sushi fish.

➢ Instead of raw fish, use poached shrimp, grilled tuna, or braised lobster tail meat.

Roasted Golden and Red Beet Salad with Goat Cheese Vinaigrette and Toasted Hazelnuts

I cannot understand why people claim they dislike beets. Beets are wonderful; they are sweet, earthy, and incredibly good for you. Roasting beets improves their flavor because it concentrates and caramelizes the sugars, but if you have to boil them, use the smallest quantity of water you can. Goat cheese and roasted beets complement each other very well, and hazelnuts beautifully accentuate the nuttiness of the beets. This salad is also really colorful and looks terrific on the plate.

If you live near a good farmers' market, you may be able to find Chioggia (or "candy cane") beets, which will make your salad even more festive.

Makes 4 servings

4 medium gold beets

4 medium red beets

¼ cup canola oil

Salt and freshly ground black pepper to taste

4 tablespoons sherry vinegar

2 tablespoons extra-virgin olive oil

½ cup mayonnaise

1 cup soft goat cheese, such as chèvre

Juice of 2 lemons

2 cups mixed baby greens

¼ cup toasted hazelnuts for garnish

Preheat the oven to 375 degrees.

Toss the gold beets in half the canola oil, and sprinkle liberally with salt and pepper. Wrap all four beets together in aluminum foil, then place on a cookie sheet. Repeat with the red beets. Bake all the beets for 30 to 45 minutes, or until you are able to pierce the beets through the foil easily with a sharp knife or a skewer.

When the beets are cool enough to handle, peel them. This is easily done: Simply rub each beet with a kitchen towel or with your hands. Careful—the red beets will stain your kitchen towel as well as your hands. Try using extra-sturdy paper towels. I always work with the golden beets first so that they don't get similarly stained, and I keep the red and gold beets separate until assembling the salad. Cut all the peeled beets into wedges, toss them with the vinegar and olive oil, and set aside.

In a separate mixing bowl, mix the mayonnaise with half the goat cheese and the lemon juice. This dressing may be a little thick; if so, thin it down with a little cold water.

When you are ready to serve the salad, toss the baby greens with the beets and the dressing. Garnish each salad with chunks of the remaining goat cheese and the toasted hazelnuts.

Options

➢ If I am serving this to someone
who isn't really fond of beets, I
disguise the salad with other ingredients like segments of oranges, some shaved fennel,
small pieces of Moroccan oil-
cured olives, and watercress. All
the flavors work really well together, but you should also experiment with other ingredients
like avocado and grapefruit.

➢ If you don't want to make a
creamy dressing, just drizzle
olive oil and lemon juice on the
salad. Other options include using a flavored oil like Cumin Oil
(page 54). Or if you're feeling
extravagant, use truffle oil. But
be careful: A little truffle oil goes
a long way. I think that if it's
overused, truffle oil starts
smelling a little like gasoline.

Thai Chopped Salad

Thai chopped meat or poultry salad is called *laab*. The fragrance and citrusy flavor of the lemongrass, lime leaf, and the freshness of the herbs make this a perfect salad for hot summer days when you don't want to be cooking for long.

Makes 4 servings

2 cups coarsely ground chicken (see Options below)

8 ounces cellophane noodles

Juice of 4 limes

2 tablespoons Thai fish sauce

1 large red onion, thinly sliced

2 jalapeño peppers, thinly sliced

2 tomatoes, seeded and thinly sliced

1 red pepper, julienned

1 carrot, julienned

1 stalk celery, cut into thin pieces

½ cup finely chopped lemongrass

4 kaffir lime leaves, finely chopped

1 ginger blossom, finely chopped

1 cup mint leaves

1 cup cilantro leaves

½ cup basil leaves

½ cup Vietnamese mint leaves (optional)

1 cup toasted peanuts (see Options below)

In a large sauté pan or wok over medium heat, sauté the chicken. Try not to brown it too much.

While the chicken browns, place the cellophane noodles in a bowl of hot water and let the noodles soak for 10 minutes. Drain, and cut with scissors into 2-inch lengths. Set aside briefly.

Transfer the chicken into a bowl and add all other ingredients except the herbs and peanuts. It is important to add the lime juice, fish sauce, and cellophane noodles while the meat is still hot. Just before serving (warm or at room temperature), toss the salad with the herbs and peanuts.

Options

➤ Try using ground pork or turkey instead of chicken. You could also use poached shrimp or fish or shellfish.

➤ Substitute peanut brittle or sesame brittle for the toasted peanuts. Use the salad as filling for a lettuce or rice paper wrap.

Seared Tuna and Three-Bean Salad

This is a variation on niçoise salad. It is really simple and versatile: It's the sort of salad I make when I have little bits of everything in the fridge, not really enough for a side dish, but when combined, plenty to make a large salad. I use fresh tuna for this salad, but a good-quality canned tuna works too. I love the spark of sweetness from the apple, but if you think it's too weird, just leave it out. You can substitute practically any other vegetables for the ones I have used.

Makes 4 servings

1 (8-ounce) piece tuna

Salt and freshly ground black pepper
   to taste

½ cup green beans, blanched

½ cup sugar snap peas, blanched

½ cup cooked white beans

½ cup cooked kidney beans

½ cup fresh fava beans, blanched

½ cup cherry tomatoes

¼ cup pitted olives

1 cup diced Fuji apple or Asian pear
   (optional)

2 tablespoons capers, rinsed

Juice and grated zest of 2 lemons

1 cup canola oil

Season the tuna well with lots of salt and pepper. Sear the tuna for 1 minute on each side on a hot grill or in a lightly oiled skillet. Remove from the heat and let the tuna rest in the refrigerator while you assemble the salad.

In a large bowl, combine the remaining ingredients. Allow the ingredients to marinate for up to a half hour in the refrigerator. Serve the salad chilled with sliced tuna.

Options

➤ Toss 8 ounces of canned tuna with the rest of the salad ingredients, and serve on slices of grilled sourdough bread for a quick lunch.

➤ Try adding grilled Yukon gold potatoes and minced scallions, and leave out some of the beans.

➤ Poach an egg (or boil an egg for 4 minutes, then peel), and serve the egg right on top of the salad. The soft yolk melts into the vinaigrette, making a delicious creamy sauce.

Rice Noodle Salad

I came up with this recipe for my restaurant AZ. I needed a "pasta" salad for one of New York's early summer Restaurant Weeks, when many restaurants around Manhattan offer a $20-or-so prix-fixe lunch menu. At the outset of the week, restaurants set up clothed tables on the sidewalk outside their establishments, where samples of signature dishes are served for a pittance, all to raise money for various good causes.

I needed to come up with something that would be inexpensive to make, easy to execute, and really yummy. Pho noodles are dried rice noodles that are used mostly for soup throughout Vietnam, Laos, and Thailand. They are very similar to the fresh chow fun noodles you find in Chinatown, but better because they're dried and will keep for ages in your pantry.

Makes 4 appetizer servings

1 one-pound bag pho noodles

1 cup canola oil

¼ cup balsamic vinegar

2 tablespoons rice wine vinegar

2 tablespoons sherry

1 tablespoon whole-grain mustard

½ cup julienned carrots

½ cup sugar snap peas

½ cup diced cucumber

½ cup diced celery

½ cup diced tart apple, such as
   Granny Smith

2 boneless skinless chicken breasts,
   poached and shredded

½ cup roughly chopped scallions

**Ground Sichuan peppercorns and
   salt to taste**

Lemon or lime juice (optional)

Bring a large pot of salted water to boil. When it is at a rolling boil, add the noodles. Blanch for a minute, then drain and shock in ice water immediately. Drain the noodles again, and toss them with a little of the canola oil.

In a mixing bowl, whisk together both vinegars, the sherry, mustard, and the remaining canola oil. A half hour before serving, toss the vegetables and apple in half the vinaigrette.

Just prior to serving add the remaining ingredients and the rest of the vinaigrette. Season judiciously and add more acid (in the form of lemon or lime juice) if desired. Serve immediately.

Note: I like to make the vinaigrette in advance and toss the still-warm noodles with Sichuan pepper, salt, and a small amount of the vinaigrette so that the noodles absorb the flavors.

Other Appetizers

Friends as well as guests at my restaurant Supa often tell me that they could quite happily live off appetizers alone. The idea that you can have three or more small servings, tasting a greater variety of things, is very appealing. I have included a wide selection of tapas and dim-sum favorites that are easy to prepare ahead of time—and great fun to make.

Scallop Ceviche with Lemongrass

This dish is redolent of lemongrass, fresh chilies, and sweet red onions and is thoroughly refreshing. Feel free to substitute a different shellfish, or even a firm whitefish. Just make sure that any fish or shellfish you use in this recipe is really fresh.

Makes 4 servings

10 large scallops

1 large jalapeño, minced

1 stalk lemongrass, tough top and bottom removed and very finely chopped

2 kaffir lime leaves (see Options below)

1 medium red onion, diced

2 cups freshly squeezed lime juice (see Options below)

¼ cup sugar

Salt and freshly ground black pepper to taste

¼ cup finely chopped cilantro leaves

¼ cup finely chopped flat parsley leaves

¼ cup finely chopped mint leaves

In a nonreactive bowl (I like using a large glass or ceramic one), add all the ingredients except the cilantro, parsley, and mint. Allow the scallops to "cook" in the marinade for at least 20 minutes. Drain off the excess liquid. Chill, then, just before serving, fold in the chopped herbs.

Options

➢ You can serve this like an hors
d'oeuvre by dicing the scallops
(in which case reduce the time
the scallops marinate), and
serving them on fried wonton
chips, or crostini. I find that the
scallops tend to fall off the
chips, so I fold a little wasabi
mayonnaise into the ceviche, to
act as an adhesive. To make
wasabi mayonnaise, combine
½ cup commercial mayonnaise,
2 teaspoons fresh lime juice,
and 1½ teaspoons prepared
wasabi paste, or to taste. Mix
thoroughly with a fork.

➢ Substitute the grated zest of
½ lime if lime leaves are
unavailable.

➢ You may substitute lemon, but
the flavor just isn't the same.

Sashimi Beef Rolls

These beef rolls make a splendid and unusual appetizer. They can be made up to 4 hours in advance and kept refrigerated. The dish is a cross between a beef carpaccio and a more traditional sushi roll. I like serving these rolls with classic pesto that has a little mayonnaise folded into it. Use a nicer cut of beef, because the beef is the star of this recipe. A mandoline will make short work of all those julienned ingredients.

Makes 4 to 6 appetizer servings

1 pound aged New York strip steak, frozen for 15 minutes (see Options below)

1 cup julienned cucumbers

1 cup julienned green apple

1 cup julienned celery

1 cup julienned scallions

½ cup julienned red peppers

½ cup julienned pickled cucumber (I like to use dill pickles)

¼ cup crumbled blue cheese (use your favorite; I like Stilton)

1 cup pea shoots (see Options below)

Slice the beef across the grain into thin pieces, making the slices as long as possible. Lay each piece on a flat surface. Place a little of each of the julienned vegetables and pickled cucumber, cheese, and pea shoots along one side and roll up the beef. The finished product should resemble a roll with bits of vegetables sticking out.

If I am not using these rolls immediately I like to brush a little canola oil on the beef to keep it from turning brown or drying. Store refrigerated for up to 4 hours under a damp, clean kitchen towel.

Options

➤ If you don't like raw beef or are unable to eat it raw, just sear the beef briefly, sliced or whole depending on how rare you want it, let cool, and make the rolls.

➤ Use tuna or salmon instead of the beef (I'd leave out the cheese if using fish).

➤ Use whatever vegetable you like in the roll. If I am feeling really lazy, I just use a couple of pieces of blanched pencil asparagus, then I cook the rolls briefly on a really hot grill and shave Parmesan cheese over the top for a quick appetizer or light lunch.

➤ If you are unable to get pea shoots, use baby lettuce.

Other Appetizers

Spicy Tuna and Mango Tartare

I never wanted my sushi recipes to be too traditional. So I've come up with some pretty eclectic sushi and *maki* rolls over the years. One of them was a spicy tuna and mango roll. The recipe for this tartare is based on that roll.

Makes 8 to 10 appetizer servings

2 cups finely diced sushi-grade tuna
½ cup finely diced really ripe mango
    (yellow with red patches, and
    fairly soft around the stem; see
    Options below)
A drop or two of Cumin Oil (page 54)
½ cup Chipotle Mayonnaise (page 70)
2 tablespoons English mustard, such
    as Coleman's
Juice of ½ lemon
Salt and freshly ground black pepper
    to taste
Rippled salted potato chips, such as
    Ruffles

Combine the tuna and mango in a bowl and add the Cumin Oil. Mix well. Add the mayonnaise, English mustard, and lemon juice, season with salt and pepper, and toss well. Transfer to a chilled bowl on a large platter. Surround the bowl with potato chips. Or, spoon a small amount of tartare on each chip and serve like an hors d'oeuvre.

Note: It is important to make sure that the raw tuna is coated with a little oil before adding the mayonnaise and acid, especially if you are not serving the tartare immediately. The oil protects the fish, preventing it from being "cooked" by the acid in the lemon juice as well as the mayonnaise. I do suggest mixing everything up only at the last moment.

Options

➤ Use a really ripe and sweet Bartlett pear instead of the mango. Whatever fruit you decide to use should have the same buttery texture as the tuna.

➤ Serve a small mound of the tartare on a salad of cucumber, radish, and avocado.

Scotch Eggs

Scotch eggs are traditionally hard-boiled eggs wrapped in sausage and fried. They were a beloved staple at my family's picnics while I was growing up. These are slightly different because instead of hard-boiling the egg, I keep mine semisoft so that when you cut open the Scotch egg, the yolk oozes out.

Makes 4 appetizer servings

4 large eggs

2 cups Spicy Lamb Sausage (page 114)

2 cups *panko* (sturdy Japanese breadcrumbs)

Canola oil for frying

Place the eggs in cold water, bring to a boil, and simmer for 3 minutes. Allow to cool in the hot water. At this point the whites should be set but the yolks will still be very runny.

Peel the eggs very carefully. Encase each egg in a thin layer of sausage. Roll in the *panko* and fry the eggs in ¼ inch of the oil until golden brown.

Options

➤ Scotch eggs are delicious on panzanelle, which is Italian bread salad (see page 2).

➤ Instead of making your own sausage, just use store-bought Italian or breakfast sausage.

Indian Chickpea Flour Fritters

These fritters make great canapés. They are a cross between a *panisse* (which is a thick, fried Provençale pancake made with chickpea flour) and a chickpea cracker. I like to serve it with creamy white bean puree (the recipe is in my first cookbook, *Cooking from A to Z*).

Makes 6 to 8 appetizer servings

2 cups water

1 herb sachet consisting of dried chili, bay leaf, black peppercorns, and curry leaves (available in Indian stores; see Ingredient Sources, page 199)

½ cup half-and-half

Salt to taste

1 cup chickpea flour

¼ cup fine cornmeal

1 medium onion, diced and caramelized

1 tablespoon mustard seeds, either gold or black or a mixture of both, toasted

1 teaspoon coarsely ground toasted coriander seeds

1 tablespoon butter

Freshly ground black pepper to taste

Canola oil for frying

In a heavy-bottomed saucepan over high heat, bring the water to a boil with the herb sachet. Simmer for 5 minutes, then add the half-and-half and a few pinches of salt and simmer for another 5 minutes. Remove the sachet. Slowly whisk in the chickpea flour and cornmeal, stirring constantly. Allow the mixture to thicken slightly. Add the caramelized onion, mustard seeds, and coriander seeds. Mix well, and add the butter. Adjust the seasoning. Remove from heat.

Spread the chickpea mixture thinly (about ⅛ inch) on a sheet pan or cookie sheet. Cool. When it has set, cut the mixture into 2 by 2-inch squares. Over medium heat, bring an inch of canola oil to 375 degrees and fry the squares until golden, about 3 to 5 minutes. Drain on paper towels and sprinkle with salt. These fritters will keep in an airtight container for up to 2 days.

Options

➤ I sometimes cut the chickpea mixture into thin strips to use as a garnish for salads or soups. They taste almost like corn tortillas.

➤ You can vary the flavoring of the chickpea mixture in any number of ways, adding ground toasted cumin seeds, a little toasted sesame oil, ground dried porcini mushrooms, grated lemon zest, what-have-you.

Smoky Eggplant and Yogurt Puree

This eggplant puree is not only delicious, it is easy to make and amazingly versatile. I think it is more Middle Eastern to achieve a velvety smooth puree, but if you prefer a chunkier blend, just pulse the mixture in the processor until you get the texture you want. The yogurt needs to be strained through cheesecloth overnight, so plan accordingly.

Makes about 3 cups

4 Japanese eggplants (or 2 Italian eggplants), stem ends sliced off

Canola oil for slicking the eggplants

1 clove garlic, chopped

Juice and grated zest of 2 lemons

1 anchovy fillet (optional)

1 tablespoon tahini (optional; see Options below)

Salt and freshly ground black pepper to taste

1 cup strained yogurt (see Note below)

1 cup finely chopped parsley

Toss the whole eggplants in a little canola oil and place on a hot grill or under a hot broiler for 10 minutes on each side. The skin will char, but that's fine. Allow the eggplants to cool, then peel off the charred skin. Discard any liquid that seeps out of the eggplant.

Place the flesh of the eggplants into the workbowl of a food processor with the garlic, lemon juice and zest, and the optional anchovy and tahini. Process until very smooth, taste carefully, and adjust the seasoning. I like to transfer it into a bowl at this point and swirl in the yogurt and parsley because I like the swirled effect, but you can just put the yogurt and parsley into the food processor to finish. Either way it will taste the same. Divide among 4 to 6 bowls, or see Options.

Note: Strained yogurt is simply plain yogurt that is strained over a bowl through cheesecloth (or a clean cotton kitchen towel) overnight. The whey escapes, leaving a thick curd similar to marscapone or fresh cheese. Measure the yogurt after straining.

Options

➢ If I don't have any tahini, I use a little peanut butter.

➢ Try adding a few pinches of Aleppo chili flakes to the mixture. It will give it a little spice and accentuate the smoky flavor. Aleppo chile is from Aleppo in Syria, mildly spicy and quite smoky. The flakes are available from Kalustyan's (see page 199).

➢ The puree can be used as a dip with crackers or flat bread or crudités.

➢ It is perfectly delicious instead of mayonnaise in a lamb sandwich.

➢ Serve it with seared scallops and a tomato vinaigrette.

Toasted Walnut, Cheese, and Chili Shortbread

These shortbreads are delicious on their own with drinks, or as part of a cheese platter.

Makes 6 to 8 appetizer servings

2 cups all-purpose flour

4 tablespoons baking powder

1 teaspoon salt

½ teaspoon chili flakes

½ cup (1 stick) cold butter, cut into 1-inch cubes

6 tablespoons grated Parmesan cheese

½ cup grated aged cheddar cheese

¼ cup toasted walnuts

Preheat the oven to 400 degrees. Using a food processor, mix the flour, baking powder, salt, and chili flakes. Add the cold butter and pulse until the mixture resembles coarse sand. Add the cheeses and walnuts and just enough cold water to bind the mixture. Remove from the food processor and roll into a log. Chill for at least an hour.

Slice the log into ¼-inch coins and place on a cookie sheet, remembering that the shortbread will spread slightly. Bake for 10 minutes or until golden brown. Will keep in an airtight container for up to 3 days.

Green Chili Spoon Bread

Spoon bread is a lovely cross between polenta and a soufflé. But it's a lot more forgiving than a soufflé, and can actually stay fluffy and light for quite a while after coming out of the oven. The spoon bread may be baked in a medium-sized casserole or in individual ramekins.

Makes 4 appetizer servings

1½ cups whole milk

1 cup fine cornmeal

1 tablespoon baking powder

1 teaspoon baking soda

1 cup corn kernels

½ cup diced roasted green chilies, such as poblanos

½ cup grated Parmigiano-Reggiano cheese

3 large eggs, separated

Salt and freshly ground black pepper to taste

Preheat the oven to 350 degrees.

In a heavy-bottomed pot over medium-low heat, bring the milk to a gentle boil, then slowly add the cornmeal, whisking constantly so that no lumps develop. Cook until the mixture thickens, then cool for 10 minutes. Add the baking powder, baking soda, corn, green chilies, and cheese, and incorporate well. Stir in the egg yolks. Whip the egg whites to soft peaks, and fold them into the cornmeal mixture. Season to taste with salt and pepper. Transfer into a well-buttered casserole and bake for 15 minutes or until the spoon bread rises and browns slightly on the top.

Meatballs and Yogurt Sauce

In the south-central Indian city of Hyderabad, there is quite a substantial Persian and Middle Eastern influence. These meatballs convey that influence. They're slightly spicy and complex in flavor.

Makes about 20 appetizer servings, 3 meatballs each

For the Meatballs

- 1 pound ground beef
- ½ pound ground veal
- ¼ pound ground pork
- 2 eggs
- 2 cups cooled steamed rice
- 1 cup caramelized chopped onion
- 1 tablespoon toasted ground coriander seeds
- 1 tablespoon toasted ground cumin seeds
- 1 tablespoon toasted ground fennel seeds
- 1 tablespoon toasted ground cardamom pods
- 1 teaspoon ground cinnamon
- 1 teaspoon ground cloves
- 2 tablespoons Aleppo chili flakes (or 2 teaspoons ground cayenne)
- Salt and freshly ground black pepper to taste
- 2 tablespoons canola oil

For the Yogurt Sauce

- 1 tablespoon flour
- 2 tablespoons unsalted butter
- ½ cup whole milk
- 2 cups whole milk yogurt

Mix together the beef, veal, pork, eggs, rice, onion, spices, salt, and pepper with your hands. Form the mixture into ¾-inch balls. In a large skillet over medium-high heat, sear and brown the meatballs in the canola oil in batches, if necessary, to avoid crowding. Reserve.

Put the flour and butter in the same skillet, and cook over medium-low heat, stirring, for 3 to 4 minutes, until the flour starts to brown. Slowly add the milk, stirring constantly to prevent any lumps from forming. Bring to a boil and simmer for 3 minutes. Raise the heat to medium, and return the meatballs to the flour mixture and cook, stirring occasionally and gently, for 5 minutes. Just before serving, stir in the yogurt, turn down the heat, and simmer for 1 minute.

Options

➤ Make the meatballs, brown them, and add them to your favorite tomato sauce. Serve over pasta.

➤ Make the meatballs slightly larger, brown them, then roast them through in a preheated 350-degree oven. Stuff into pita bread with julienned romaine, tomato, and, if you like, white bean puree or eggplant puree.

➤ Form into hamburger patties and serve on grilled hamburger buns with sliced onion, tomato, and pickle.

Buttermilk-Marinated Chicken Livers with Haricots Verts Salad

I always disliked liver—until I tasted this salad. The richness of the chicken livers, the crunch of the haricots verts, and the acidic sweetness of the vinaigrette complement one another beautifully.

Makes 4 appetizer servings

½ **pound chicken or duck livers, fat and veins removed, well rinsed**

1 **cup buttermilk**

1 **onion, cut into small dice**

1 **clove garlic, finely chopped**

1 **tablespoon chopped fresh thyme leaves**

½ **cup sherry vinegar**

2 **tablespoons smooth Dijon mustard**

1 **cup olive oil**

Salt and freshly ground black pepper to taste

½ **cup all-purpose flour**

1 **egg, well beaten**

1 **cup unflavored dry bread crumbs (I like using *panko*, which is a sturdy Japanese bread crumb)**

3 **tablespoons clarified butter (or ghee)**

2 **cups lightly blanched haricots verts (see Options below)**

Pat the livers dry with paper towels and soak them in the buttermilk for up to 6 hours.

While the livers are soaking, make the vinaigrette: In a roomy skillet, caramelize the diced onion until it turns mahogany. Add the garlic and thyme and continue cooking for a further 3 to 4 minutes. Deglaze with the sherry vinegar. Whisk in the mustard and olive oil. Season and set aside.

Drain the livers and pat them dry. Place the flour in one bowl, the beaten egg in a second bowl, and put the bread crumbs in a third bowl. Dip the livers in the flour, shaking off any excess, then dip them into the egg, and finally into the bread crumbs. In another skillet over medium heat, fry the livers in

the clarified butter until the livers
turn golden brown.

Toss the haricots verts and vinaigrette together. Scatter the livers on
the salad, and serve.

Options

➢ Haricots verts works best for
this salad, but young and tender
green beans are good too.

➢ I sometimes toss diced Fuji apples or Asian pears into the
salad for a sweet counterpoint
as well as additional crunch.

➢ Make a lovely salad with roasted
golden beets, sautéed liver,
arugula or watercress, and
chunks of goat cheese.

➢ Wrap the fried chicken livers
with partially cooked and cooled
bacon, fastening with a toothpick if necessary. Glaze the bacon with Pomegranate Glaze
(page 65), and bake in a preheated 350-degree oven for
10 minutes, or until 1 bacon is
sizzling.

Minced Pork and Prawn Wrapped in Tofu Skin

Tofu skins can be bought fresh in Chinese supermarkets. They are very commonly encountered in Chinese and Japanese vegetarian cuisine. It is especially great for vegans, because it is made purely of soy. Most sheets of tofu skin that I've seen are 3 feet by 3 feet. For this recipe, the sheets should be cut into 1-foot squares.

Makes 4 to 8 appetizer servings

For the Filling

- ½ cup minced pork
- ½ cup small pieces peeled shrimp
- ¼ cup chopped water chestnuts
- 2 scallions, green part only, cut into small pieces
- 2 tablespoons soy sauce
- 1 teaspoon Thai fish sauce
- Salt and freshly ground black pepper to taste

- Canola oil for frying
- 1 large sheet tofu skin, cut into 1-foot squares

Preheat the oven to 350 degrees.

Mix all the ingredients for the filling together. Sauté a scant tablespoon of the filling in a bit of the oil and taste it carefully to make sure it is seasoned properly, adjusting if you need to.

Place the tofu skin on a flat surface and spread the filling evenly all over the skin. Roll it up like a jelly roll. Fry in canola oil until golden brown, about 10 minutes. Bake for about 5 minutes to cook the center of the roll. Cut crosswise into rounds and serve immediately.

Options

➢ If you can't find fresh, canned water chestnuts work very well.

➢ If you can't find tofu skins, just use 6 sheets of phyllo dough (follow the instructions on the box).

➢ Instead of frying the roll, bake for 20 minutes in a preheated 350-degree oven.

➢ I like serving this with a ginger-and-chili sauce, but one of my sous-chefs uses a spicy tomato ketchup (ketchup with lots of *sambal*, a heady Indonesian spice blend, added), which is just as good.

Eggplant and Shrimp "Toasts"

Shrimp toast is a staple of dim sum. It is traditionally made by sandwiching white bread with shrimp mousse, then pan-frying or deep-frying it. In this version, Asian eggplant substitutes for the bread. Do not overstuff the sandwiches because the center will not cook through if the sandwich is too thick.

Makes about 8 appetizer servings

2 cups cleaned medium shrimp

2 tablespoons finely chopped ginger

2 tablespoons heavy cream

¼ cup finely minced scallions

2 tablespoons Thai fish sauce

Salt and freshly ground black pepper to taste

2 Asian eggplants

Flour for dredging

2 eggs

1 cup dry bread crumbs, preferably *panko* (sturdy Japanese bread crumbs)

Neutral oil for frying or deep-frying

Sesame Salt (page 53)

In a food processor, pulse the shrimp just until there are still large pieces; the different textures are important in this recipe. Remove the shrimp to a large bowl and fold in the ginger, cream, and scallions. Season with the fish sauce, salt, and pepper. Keep refrigerated.

Cut the eggplants into 3-inch rounds, about ½ inch thick. Divide the shrimp mixture among half the eggplant slices, and cover with the remaining eggplant slices. In one bowl, place the flour; in a second, beat the eggs well; and in a third, put the bread crumbs. Dust the eggplant sandwiches with flour, then dip them into the beaten eggs, and finally dredge them in the bread crumbs. Sauté the eggplant sand-

wiches in a large sauté pan over
medium-high heat, or deep-fry until
golden brown. Season with toasted
Sesame Salt.

Options

➤ Instead of shrimp mousse, make
the dish vegetarian by using
thick hummus or curried lentil
puree (recipe on page 23 in
Cooking from A to Z).

Shrimp and Julienned Vegetable—Filled Tofu

When I was a child, my Sixth Auntie would always bring a platter of these delicious filled tofu for family gatherings. They were always served with a sweet-tart peanut and tamarind sauce. In the markets of Southeast Asia, you can buy fried tofu puffs, threaded onto a strand, like pearls on a necklace. In American markets, you usually find these fried tofu puffs in the frozen food section, but if you happen to live in an area with a large Asian community, you will find them fresh. An alternative is to use Japanese tofu pouches, called tofu puffs.

Makes 12 appetizer servings

12 tofu puffs

12 large poached shrimp, cut into small pieces (see Options below)

½ cup julienned cucumber

½ cup julienned celery

¼ cup julienned scallions, green parts only

¼ cup blanched bean sprouts

Toss all the ingredients together and stuff into tofu puffs. Serve with side of Chunky Peanut-Tamarind Sauce (page 85).

Options

➤ Consider using cold roasted pork or chicken instead of (or in addition to) shrimp.

➤ Try filling the pouches with your favorite sandwich filling: tuna salad, chicken salad, or even egg salad.

➤ For a quick sushi-style appetizer or light lunch, fill the puffs with a salad of diced sushi-grade tuna, some sushi rice, and avocado.

➤ Other vegetables may be used, like roasted eggplant, grilled zucchini, roasted asparagus, and/or diced avocado. Just use your favorites or whatever is in season.

Oyster Vichyssoise

Vichyssoise is traditionally made with leeks and potatoes, and is usually served chilled. I am not really fond of chilled soup—somehow it seems a little wrong. So I serve this vichyssoise hot with a little cold crème fraîche. Given the celebrated aphrodisiac quality of oysters, this is a soup I like to serve as a first course for a Valentine's Day menu.

Makes 4 servings

2 cups sliced leeks (wash thoroughly to remove any grit) (see Options below)

Butter

3 potatoes, peeled and roughly diced

4 cups chicken stock

1 teaspoon fresh thyme leaves

1 cup shucked oysters with their liquid

Salt and freshly ground black pepper to taste

Crème fraîche for garnish

Sweat the leeks in a little butter until very tender, but be sure they don't brown. Add the potatoes, chicken stock, and thyme. Bring to a boil and simmer for 20 minutes or until the potatoes are tender. Add the oysters and puree the soup in a blender or with an immersion blender. Strain through a fine strainer. Season. Serve hot with a nice blob of crème fraîche.

Options

➢ Instead of leeks, use fennel in the soup and finish with a splash of Pernod.

➢ If you do not want to puree the oysters, gently poach them in the soup for a minute and serve.

➢ Reserve 4 large oysters, dip them in seasoned cornmeal, and fry them in clarified butter. Serve as a garnish for the soup.

Lamb and Potato Samosas

I love "street food." Samosas are sold all over Asia, anywhere there is an Indian community. The curry flavor of the filling gives it an Indian accent, but if you dislike curry, leave it out and basically you have an empanada or a turnover.

This is a basic dough that's flavored with coriander and Aleppo chili powder. Made from a Syrian chile, Aleppo chili powder imparts a lovely smoky flavor. I sometimes add a little chickpea flour to the mixture because it gives the dough a nice nutty flavor.

Makes about 10 small appetizer servings

For the Samosa Dough

- **1 cup all-purpose flour**
- **2 tablespoons baking powder**
- **2 tablespoons Aleppo chili powder**
- **2 tablespoons toasted coriander seeds, crushed with a mortar and pestle**
- **1 cup (2 sticks) butter, chilled and diced**
- **¼ cup water**

In the workbowl of a food processor, combine all the dry ingredients. Add the diced butter, and pulse the mixture just until it resembles coarse sand. Slowly add the water until the dough comes together in a lump. Wrap the dough in plastic and let it rest for a half hour.

For the Filling

- **1 tablespoon Javin curry powder**
- **1 tablespoon Madras curry powder**
- **1 tablespoon Garam Masala (page 55)**
- **2 cups diced lamb, from the leg**
- **2 tablespoons canola oil**
- **1 large onion, diced**
- **¼ cup peeled and diced ginger**
- **4 large cloves garlic, peeled and roughly chopped**
- **1 large russet potato, peeled and diced**
- **2 Yukon gold potatoes, peeled and diced**
- **2 tablespoons tomato paste**
- **½ cup water or white wine**
- **¼ cup chopped cilantro leaves**
- **Canola oil for frying**

Mix the curry powders and Garam Masala, and toss the diced lamb in the mixture. In a heavy-bottomed deep skillet or saucepan over high heat, brown the lamb in the canola oil. Remove the lamb from the skillet. Add the onion, ginger, and garlic to the skillet, and stir until the vegetables are caramelized. Return the lamb to the skillet and add the potatoes and tomato paste. Stir in the water or wine and cook over very low heat until the potatoes are soft and most of the liquid has evaporated, stirring occasionally, about 10 to 15 minutes. Remove from the heat and let cool. Just before making the Samosas, fold in the coriander leaves.

Roll out the dough into ¼-inch-thick sheets and, with a 4-inch cylinder or cookie cutter, cut into 4-inch circles. Place a large spoonful of the filling in the center of each circle, fold the dough over, crimp it, and set aside. Repeat until all of the filling is used up. Fry the Samosas until golden brown in 1 inch of canola oil over high heat. Serve immediately with your favorite prepared chutney.

Options

➤ I often substitute ¼ cup chickpea flour for ¼ cup regular flour in the recipe for the crust, to give the crust hefty texture and a depth of flavor.

➤ If you don't want to make your own dough, use store-bought frozen puff pastry or phyllo dough. Simply follow the instructions on the box.

➤ You can make the filling vegetarian by substituting cauliflower or peas for the lamb.

➤ Samosas are traditionally fried, but they are just as good baked in a preheated 350-degree oven for about 15 minutes.

➤ Use the filling to make a shepherd's pie: Put the filling into a gratin pan, top with mashed potatoes, dot with butter, and sprinkle with cheese. Bake in a preheated 350-degree oven until heated through and the cheese is browned.

Marinades, Rubs, and Condiments

Basic Five-Spice Powder

You can buy ready-made five-spice mixture from the supermarket, and some-times it's actually good. The problem with premixed spices is that one has no idea how long the mixture has been in the tin. I like being able to make my own, simply because you have control of the quantity of each ingredient. For exam-ple, I'm not particularly fond of cloves (I find them too cloying), so my mixture has a scant amount, but I do like the peppery flavor of Sichuan pepper, so I use more, especially now that the ban on imported Sichuan peppercorns has been lifted—provided the peppercorns have been heated to 140 degrees for 10 min-utes to destroy the cankers that attack citrus plants. You should make similar adjustments according to your particular taste. This is just a guideline, as are all the recipes in this book.

Makes about ½ cup

2 tablespoons toasted fennel seeds

2 tablespoons toasted coriander seeds

1 large cinnamon stick

1 teaspoon ground cloves

3 tablespoons toasted Sichuan peppercorns

2 tablespoons black peppercorns

1 tablespoon white peppercorns

Grind all the spices together on a spice grinder or with a mortar and pestle, then sift the mixture to get rid of any stray large pieces. Store in an airtight container for up to 3 months. A can or tin is preferable because it will keep out the light, which affects the spice.

Sesame Salt

Sesame Salt is a staple in Korean kitchens. It is really simple to make and a little goes a long way. Do not make too much at one time. The high oil content of sesame seeds makes them prone to turning rancid. By the way, we keep sesame seeds—and poppy seeds and pine nuts—in the freezer.

Makes about 3 cups

2 cups sesame seeds

1 cup kosher salt

Put an 8-inch cast-iron sauté pan over medium heat. Add the sesame seeds and kosher salt. Toast, stirring constantly, until the sesame seeds are golden.

Marinades, Rubs, and Condiments

Cumin Oil

Flavored oils are a really quick and easy way to add flavor to a dish. This is a recipe for Cumin Oil, but you can really substitute any other spice you would prefer.

Makes about ¼ cup

2 tablespoons toasted coarsely
**   ground cumin seeds**
¼ cup canola oil
1 clove garlic, smashed

Combine the ingredients in a small saucepan over low heat. Simmer for 2 to 3 minutes. Cool, then strain through a cheesecloth. Store, refrigerated, for up to 1 month.

Options

➢ Use the same procedure, with or without the garlic, with other spices like toasted coriander seeds, black peppercorns and bay leaf, dried thyme and lavender, or even a vanilla pod.

➢ Use the flavored oil in a vinaigrette instead of olive oil.

➢ Add the flavored oil—or half-flavored, half-unflavored oil—to a mayonnaise instead of plain canola oil.

➢ Lobster salad with avocado, tomato, and a little vanilla oil (see first Option) is great.

Masala: Indian Spice Marinade and Its Many Forms

There was a vegetarian restaurant called Dewi Annapur in Kuala Lumpur that I absolutely loved. I don't know if it's still there, but if it is, anyone visiting Kuala Lumpur should have at least one meal there. There was no menu because it was run by volunteers and home cooks, and one was never sure who would show up or what they would cook. It was there that I learned about the sophistication, subtle flavors, and nuances of spices in Indian cuisine.

Garam Masala

Garam Masala is the most basic of all the masalas (masala in Hindi simply means spices). It is what we normally think of as curry powder.

Makes a little over 1 cup

¼ **cup toasted coriander seeds, finely ground**

¼ **cup toasted cumin seeds, finely ground**

¼ **cup toasted cardamom pods, finely ground**

2 tablespoons ground turmeric

2 tablespoons ground cayenne

2 tablespoons ground cinnamon

2 tablespoons ground fennel seeds

2 tablespoons ground anise seeds

Mix well and store in an airtight container for up to a month.

Tandoori Masala

Tandoori Masala is the spice mix that is generally used when meats or fish are roasted in a tandoori oven. The mixture usually includes some yogurt, which helps tenderize the meat and gives it a lovely tangy flavor. I like to drain my yogurt in cheesecloth for at least an hour to get rid of the excess liquid—overnight draining is even better.

Makes a little over 1 cup

1 cup whole-milk yogurt
2 tablespoons diced ginger
4 cloves garlic, finely chopped
1 teaspoon cayenne pepper
1 teaspoon paprika
1 tablespoon curry powder (see Options below)
Salt and freshly ground black pepper to taste

Blend the ingredients together. Marinate your meat in the masala for up to 2 hours. Remove the excess marinade from the meat and grill or roast in a very hot oven.

Options

➢ Add some Garam Masala to a batch of lentil soup, and serve with a big spoonful of yogurt.

➢ Toast some Garam Masala powder in a little neutral oil until fragrant before adding to stock or liquids.

➢ If you toss meat or vegetables in some Garam Masala before cooking, the masala needs to be browned carefully in a dry skillet. Similarly, adding "raw" curry powder to a sauce will result in a granular, raw flavor.

➤ Remove the seeds and white membranes from the jalapeño peppers if you do not want your Green Masala (page 58) too spicy.

➤ Sauté some Green Masala in a little canola oil, then carefully add white wine. Use this to steam mussels or clams. Serve with crusty bread.

➤ Rub some Green Masala on "steak fish," like swordfish or marlin, before grilling.

➤ If you find your Masala has produced a curry that is too spicy, try adding a little sweetener. I like adding a ripe banana, which not only rounds out the flavors in the curry, it also thickens the mixture, giving it an almost creamy texture.

➤ Use your favorite blend of curry powder for the Tandoori Masala. I like Madras curry powder.

➤ Toss sliced vegetables with some Tandoori Masala, then grill.

Marinades, Rubs, and Condiments

Green Masala

Green Masala is an intriguing combination of dried spices with fresh herbs and chilies. It reminds me a little of certain Thai curry mixes, but without the citric quality. This masala should be made in small batches because the fresh herbs won't keep. In countries like Malaysia, Singapore, and Thailand, it's possible to get the masala ground for you at a market, and there is usually a vendor who will make you any combination you desire. This Green Masala is particularly good with fish and shellfish.

Makes about 1 cup

2 fresh jalapeño peppers (see Options on page 57)

2 large bunches cilantro, well-washed roots, stems, and leaves

2 cups mint leaves

¼ cup chopped ginger

Grated zest of 3 limes

2 cloves garlic

¼ cup ground toasted coriander seeds

10 toasted cardamom pods

Puree all the ingredients together. The paste should be as smooth as possible. If you have the time, try making the puree with a mortar and pestle.

Mint Pesto

I don't think of this as a real pesto, more like a cross between a pesto and an Indian coriander-mint chutney. I don't add cheese to this puree, but feel free to do so if you like. I think that the fat from the cheese interferes with the bright, fresh taste of the mint.

Makes about 2½ cups

2 cups mint leaves

1 cup flat-leaf parsley leaves

1 cup toasted pine nuts

1 clove garlic

½ cup canola oil

Roughly chop the mint and parsley and place them in the workbowl of a food processor. Add the pine nuts and garlic and process until nearly pureed (I like keeping the mixture slightly chunky). Drizzle in the canola oil and pulse until just blended.

Corn Salsa

This is among the very first things I made in a professional kitchen. One of my jobs as the salad maker at Miracle Grill was to make all the salsas that we used in the restaurant, and we went through a lot of salsa. Make this recipe only when corn is at its sweetest during the peak of summer. I roast the corn in its husk before cutting the kernels off the cob, but you could just sauté the raw kernels in a little canola oil. I don't suggest blanching the corn, however, because I think it loses some of its flavor.

Makes about 2 cups

5 ears corn (see Options below)

1 red onion, finely diced

2 jalapeño peppers, finely chopped

1 red pepper, diced (see Options below)

1 cup cilantro leaves (see Options below)

Juice of 1 lime

2 tablespoons canola oil

Salt and freshly ground black pepper to taste

Preheat the oven to 300 degrees.

Remove the silk from the corn, pull the husks closed again, and roast in the oven for 30 minutes. Discard the husks and cut the corn off the cob with a sharp paring knife. Blend with the remaining ingredients in a medium bowl and taste for seasoning.

Options

➤ Corn and tarragon make a really nice combination, but if I were using tarragon I'd leave out the onion and red pepper.

➤ I like the taste and texture of raw red pepper in this salsa, but if you prefer, use diced roasted red peppers instead.

➤ If you dislike cilantro, just substitute your favorite herb—perhaps parsley, basil, or mint.

➤ This salsa makes a great dip for tortilla chips, but I find it really annoying that the kernels keep rolling off the chip because there is no binder or thickening agent to hold the salsa together. If you are serving the salsa with chips, try folding in a small amount of sour cream just so the kernels don't roll away.

Marinades, Rubs, and Condiments

Preserved Lemons

Most people think of Preserved Lemons as being strictly Moroccan, but Preserved Lemons and limes are used throughout Asia, from China to India. My grandmother used to make a delicious duck and Chinese mustard soup with preserved limes for holidays and special occasions like birthdays. My mother and Fourth Aunt carry on that tradition to this day, making a large batch of Preserved Lemons at the peak of lemon season.

Makes 10 preserved lemons

10 large lemons, well scrubbed

4 cups kosher salt (regular table salt has a bitterness that doesn't work well for this recipe)

2 cups sugar (see Options below)

2 bay leaves

2 large sprigs thyme

Juice of 5 lemons

You will need a large sealable glass jar for this, such as a 1½-quart mason jar with a clamp and rubber gasket (sealing ring). Wash the jar thoroughly in hot soapy water, rinse it well, and air-dry it.

Cut the lemons into quarters, leaving one end intact to join the quarters. Mix the salt and sugar well, and toss the cut lemons with the mixture. Tightly fill the dry glass jar with the cut lemons then poke in the bay leaves and thyme springs. Finally, pour lemon juice over all.

Cover the top of the jar with parchment, place the gasket over the parchment around the lip of the jar, and clamp the lid in place. Shake the jar well, and store in a cool place for 1 week, turning the jar from time to time. After 1 week the lemons will be ready to use. Be careful when removing lemons from the jar: Always use a clean spoon or clean hands. The Preserved Lemons will keep for up to a year, refrigerated or not.

Options

➤ Add a little honey to the recipe to mellow out the salt.

➤ If you want to speed up the curing process, freeze the quartered lemons before packing them with salt and sugar.

➤ Try substituting rosemary spears for the thyme sprigs.

Maple Vinaigrette

I like using a sweet vinaigrette, especially if it's for a dish that's being paired with spicy foods. The maple in this vinaigrette mellows out the spiciness of the tandoori spices and the smokiness from the grill. If you plan on keeping the vinaigrette for any length of time, strain out the shallots and discard. (The shallots tend to oxidize, causing the vinaigrette to spoil a lot faster.)

Makes over 2 cups

½ cup maple sugar

¼ cup white wine vinegar

¼ cup rice wine vinegar

1 tablespoon Dijon mustard

1 shallot, finely diced

1½ cups canola oil

Whisk all the ingredients together until they're emulsified.

Pomegranate Glaze

The pomegranate is a very important fruit throughout India and parts of the Middle East. One of my favorite Middle Eastern condiments is pomegranate molasses, a thick syrup that is tart, sweet, and packed with flavor. I developed this glaze for a hake dish but it could be used with any kind of fish or shellfish, or with chicken or pork.

Makes 1¼ to 1½ cups

1 cup pomegranate juice

½ cup pomegranate molasses

½ cup honey

½ cup Dijon mustard

In a small heavy-bottomed saucepan over very low heat, reduce the first three ingredients together for 45 minutes, stirring occasionally. Whisk in the Dijon mustard. The glaze will keep for a month, refrigerated.

Options

➢ Use this glaze on any meat or firm white fish.

➢ Add vinegar and olive oil for a fruity vinaigrette that's great with grilled eggplant and crumbled feta cheese. Garnish the plate with pomegranate seeds.

Carrot Tahini

This condiment makes the perfect foil for rich fried foods like Indian Chickpea Flour Fritters (page 32).

Makes about 1½ cups

½ cup tahini

¼ cup peanut butter

2 tablespoons honey

1 tablespoon *sambal* (Indonesian spice blend, available in most Asian markets)

2 tablespoons unseasoned rice vinegar

1 cup grated carrot

¼ cup chopped mint leaves

Salt and freshly ground black pepper to taste

Combine the ingredients in a medium bowl. Correct the seasoning if necessary.

Sweet and Spicy Mustard Sauce

This sauce is like a light and foamy savory sabayon. Be careful when you're whisking the yolks, because if the heat is too high, you'll have sweet-and-sour scrambled eggs! When I worked with Bobby Flay at Mesa Grill, he would tease me constantly about wanting me to make him spring rolls and hot and spicy mustard sauce. He is the reason I developed this recipe.

Makes 2 cups

3 egg yolks

¼ cup rice wine vinegar

4 tablespoons sugar (see Options below)

½ cup Coleman's English mustard powder

4 tablespoons water

¼ cup Dijon mustard

¼ cup whole-grain mustard

Salt (optional)

In a metal bowl over simmering water in a double boiler, whisk the egg yolks, vinegar, and sugar until they are pale yellow and start to ribbon, 5 to 7 minutes.

In a separate bowl, make a paste with the mustard powder and water. Add the Dijon and whole-grain mustard. Fold in the yolk mixture. Adjust the seasoning, adding a little salt if necessary.

Cool, then keep refrigerated in an airtight container for up to a week.

Options

➤ Use 4 tablespoons of honey instead of the sugar.

➤ This mustard is a wonderfully versatile condiment. Try slathering it on a roast beef and red onion sandwich. Serve it with sharp cheddar cheese and baguette slices. Try dressing a mild poached fish fillet with it. Use it as a condiment with raclette or meat fondue.

➤ Present 1 cup of the mustard in a pretty covered jar to the host at the next dinner party you attend.

Red Pepper Marmalade

This particular marmalade is a marriage of something I tasted while in Bangkok and the result of having lots of scraps from julienned red peppers at the restaurant. At almost every street-side noodle shop in Thailand, they serve a really spicy, sweet-tart but pungent condiment. This marmalade is a toned-down version of this condiment. We put a little shrimp paste in our marmalade, but leave it out if you can't find it or are allergic to shellfish. The marmalade will keep for up to a month refrigerated and tightly covered, so make more than you need for one meal, because you will want to use it over and over.

Makes 3 to 4 cups depending on the size of the red peppers

5 red bell peppers, seeded and roughly chopped

5 jalapeño peppers, seeded and chopped

10 cloves garlic, peeled and chopped

5 shallots, peeled and chopped

2 tablespoons tomato paste

¼ cup red wine vinegar

½ cup sugar

2 tablespoons shrimp paste (optional; substitute ¼ cup Thai fish sauce)

¼ cup canola oil

Salt to taste

In a standing blender, roughly buzz all the ingredients except the oil and salt. Heat the oil in a heavy-bottomed saucepan over medium heat, then add the blended ingredients and the salt. Bring to a boil, 8 to 10 minutes, turn down the heat and simmer, stirring from time to time, until the mixture begins to thicken. As the mixture reduces, you'll need to stir it more and more often to prevent it from sticking to the bottom of the pan and scorching. Keep cooking until the oil starts to separate from the marmalade. This will take between a half hour and 45 minutes.

Taste carefully and adjust the seasoning, adding salt and more vinegar or sugar if desired. Cool, then refrigerate in an airtight container for up to a month. The marmalade will thicken further during that time.

Option

➤ If you prefer the marmalade to be less spicy, remove the seeds and white ribs from the jalapeño peppers.

Chipotle Mayonnaise

A chipotle is a smoked, spicy, dried jalapeño pepper commonly used in Mexican and Southwestern cuisine. Because the jalapeños are dried, their heat is more concentrated. Although it is possible to buy them dried, I suggest using canned chipotles in adobo sauce (my favorite brand is La Morena).

Makes about 1 cup

1 egg yolk

2 tablespoons water

Juice of ½ lemon

1 cup canola oil

2 tablespoons chipotle pepper puree (simply puree 2 to 3 canned chipotles)

Salt to taste

Place the egg yolk in a small bowl, and add the water and lemon juice. With a handheld whisk, beat the yolk until pale yellow, then add the canola oil, a drop at a time, whisking constantly. Once the mixture has begun to emulsify, you can drizzle the oil in at a greater speed. Finally, fold in the chipotle puree and taste for salt.

Note: My general rule in making mayonnaise is to use 1 yolk per 1 cup of oil. Unless I want my mayonnaise to taste like olive oil, I generally use canola oil, or a mixture of canola and olive oil. My theory is that good olive oil should not be wasted on strongly flavored sauces or dressings, because the olive flavor will be masked. If you think your emulsion is about to break (you can tell because it becomes really shiny and oily in appearance), add a tablespoon of cold water and whisk like mad. It will help it reemulsify.

Options

➤ If you don't want to make mayonnaise because you're nervous about using raw eggs, simply fold the puree into commercial mayonnaise, which is made using pasteurized eggs—eggs that have been heat-treated to kill bacteria, including salmonella.

➤ Use another flavoring instead of chipotle. Some of my favorite mayonnaises are flavored with green olive tapanade, Harissa (page 72), blue cheese, or other store-bought condiments.

➤ Use this mayonnaise in a sandwich: Thinly sliced grilled steak, grilled onions, tomato, and chipotle mayonnaise on crusty sourdough bread is yummy, a great hit at Super Bowl parties.

Marinades, Rubs, and Condiments

Harissa

Harissa is a not really an Asian condiment, it is North African—Moroccan, to be specific. I use it a great deal in my recipes because it is quite similar to some of the Indian masala mixes, just slightly sweeter because of the use of roasted red bell peppers. You can vary the heat in the mixture by varying the amount of roasted poblano chilies used.

Makes about 1½ cups

4 large red bell peppers, roasted and peeled

4 poblano chilies, roasted and peeled

4 cloves garlic, peeled (see Options below)

1 Preserved Lemon (page 62), zest and rind only, finely chopped

1 cup olive oil

1 cup toasted ground coriander seeds

¼ cup toasted ground cumin seeds

Salt and freshly ground black pepper to taste

1 tablespoon honey (optional)

Combine all the peppers, garlic, and Preserved Lemon in the workbowl of a food processor. Puree 3 to 5 minutes until smooth, scraping down the side of the processor bowl with a rubber spatula two to three times. For the last minute of processing, drizzle in the olive oil in a steady stream and emulsify the mixture. Fold in the ground spices by hand. Season with salt and pepper. If you'd like the mixture to be a little less piquant, stir in 1 tablespoon of honey.

Harissa will keep in an airtight container in the refrigerator for up to 2 weeks. Remember that the flavors of the spices tend to bloom the longer the harissa sits, so if you are using the harissa after 2 weeks, be sure to taste it first.

Options

➤ I sometimes use roasted garlic instead of raw for a smoother, sweeter product.

➤ If you can get Spanish paprika in your local store, add ¼ cup to the mixture. You may need to increase the quantity of oil you use. The Spanish paprika lends a wonderful smoky flavor. Use sweet, bittersweet, or hot, as you wish.

➤ Don't think of Harissa as just a condiment. Fold a little Harissa into some mayonnaise for a great sandwich spread. I sometimes add a little to vegetable soup to make it a little richer, the way rouille is used to garnish and enrich bouillabaisse. I even make Harissa into a delicious salad dressing by whisking in some acid—fresh lemon juice or white wine vinegar.

Chermoula

Yet another North African condiment, Chermoula is coriander and lemon-based, which makes it particularly toothsome with fish and shellfish. Chermoula is quite versatile, actually: It has the ability to perk up the flavors of a mild fish like mahimahi or it can make a game fish like marlin less gamy. You will notice that I use pureed pineapple in the recipe. Besides adding sweetness and fruitiness to the recipe, fresh pineapple also has an enzyme that tenderizes meat. If you use it with fish, don't allow the fish to marinate for too long; but on the other hand, a lean piece of beef like flank steak would benefit from quite a lengthy marination. Root vegetables like potatoes or parsnips are particularly yummy if they're tossed with Chermoula before a good roasting.

Makes about 3 cups

2 cups cilantro leaves

2 Preserved Lemons (page 62)

Grated zest and juice of 2 lemons

1 cup fresh pineapple puree

1 cup toasted coriander seeds,
   ground

¼ cup paprika (I prefer Spanish
   because it is lovely and smoky)

2 tablespoons cayenne

1 cup extra-virgin olive oil

Chop the cilantro leaves and Preserved Lemons, then combine thoroughly with the remaining ingredients in a roomy bowl. This marinade will not keep, but it is so simple to assemble you can make it fresh every time you want it.

Compound Butters

Like flavored oils, compound butters are a good way to infuse foods with flavor. They keep for up to a month in the freezer, rolled into logs, wrapped in parchment or waxed paper, then tightly in foil. Make sure to label and date your compound butters, especially if you freeze more than one variety. Here are a few of my favorites, but there's no end to the variations you can come up with.

Lemon Butter
Makes about 1 cup

1 cup lemon juice

Grated zest of 2 lemons

1 cup (2 sticks) unsalted butter, softened

Salt and freshly ground black pepper to taste

In a small nonreactive saucepan over medium heat, reduce the lemon juice by half. Let cool, then pour into the workbowl of a food processor with the zest, butter, salt, and pepper. Pulse until well blended. Roll into logs.

Porcini and Sherry Butter
Makes about 2 cups

¼ cup dried porcini

½ cup warm water

½ cup sherry

2 tablespoons chopped thyme

1 shallot, diced

2 tablespoons sherry vinegar

Salt and freshly ground black pepper
    to taste

1 cup (2 sticks) unsalted butter,
    softened

Simmer the dried mushrooms, water, and sherry together until the mushrooms are tender and the liquid has reduced by a quarter. Cool, drain, and chop the mushrooms well. Place the mushrooms, their liquid, thyme, shallot, sherry vinegar, salt, pepper, and butter in the workbowl of a food processor. Pulse until well blended. Roll into logs.

Orange Honey Butter

Makes about 2 cups

2 cups orange juice

½ cup honey

Zest of 2 oranges

**1 cup (2 sticks) unsalted butter,
    softened**

Salt to taste

In a small nonreactive saucepan over medium heat, reduce the orange juice by three-quarters. Stir in the honey, zest, and salt, and let cool. Blend with butter and roll into logs.

Anchovy Butter

Makes about 1¼ cups

4 anchovy fillets

½ cup milk

2 shallots, finely diced

1 clove garlic, finely diced

Juice of 1 lemon

**1 cup (2 sticks) unsalted butter,
    softened**

Soak the anchovy fillets in the milk for half an hour. Drain them, squeeze them dry, and place them in the workbowl of a food processor. Pulse to mince the anchovies, then add the shallots, garlic, lemon juice, and butter. Pulse until well combined. Roll into logs.

Honey-Miso Dip

As strange as the mixture may sound, honey and miso go really well together. The salty-sweet quality of fermented soybeans is greatly enhanced by the use of just a bit of honey. I use quite a lot of honey in cooking because I like its consistency, especially for a dip. To counteract the sweetness, I generally use a splash of acid—in this case, rice wine vinegar.

Makes nearly 2 cups

1 cup pale miso

½ cup honey

¼ cup rice wine vinegar

Salt and freshly ground black pepper
    to taste

In a standing blender, combine all the ingredients and puree well.

Options

➤ I marinate eggplant in this mix before grilling it. A word of caution, however: The honey burns quite easily, so the eggplant must be cooked over low heat, or on a cooler part of the grill.

➤ This glaze is also delicious on oily fish like salmon. Preheat the oven to 350 degrees. Brush the top of a thick salmon steak with some Honey-Miso Dip, then bake it for 7 to 10 minutes, depending on how you like your fish cooked.

Tina's Pickled Eggplant

Pickles are one of my favorite condiments. The sweet-tart spiciness is just what we all need to wake up our palates and spark up a dish. We were serving an open-faced lamb sandwich at PAZO, and rather than serving it with the ubiquitous grilled eggplant, my chef de cuisine at both PAZO and AZ, Pino Maffeo, gave me his mother Tina's recipe for pickled eggplant. I love it so much that it's always part of my regular pantry. These pickles will keep for up to a month in an airtight jar in a cool place, but ours never seem to last that long. Instead of using Italian eggplant, we use Japanese, which I find is less spongy. If you are able to find Thai pea eggplants, they are even better.

5 large purple Japanese eggplants

4 large jalapeño peppers

4 cups vinegar (I use a mixture of half white wine and half rice wine vinegars)

1 cup sugar

1 cup packed mint leaves

½ cup salt

Cut the eggplants into bite-sized pieces. I like cutting them into ¼-inch rounds. Toss the eggplants with the salt and place in a colander with a weight on top (I use a dish that fits perfectly into the colander). Allow the eggplants to drain for up to an hour.

Slice the jalapeños into rounds, leaving the seeds in. Bring the vinegar, sugar, and salt to a boil over medium-high heat, and remove from the heat as soon as the sugar has melted. Pat the eggplant slices dry, and pack them into a large glass mason jar, tucking the mint leaves and jalapeño rounds between the layers of eggplants. Pour the hot vinegar over all, seal the jar, and keep refrigerated. The pickled eggplant rounds are ready after 1 day, but better after 3 days. They will keep, refrigerated, for 4 to 5 weeks.

Marinades, Rubs, and Condiments

Lemon-Raisin Chutney

This is one of my favorite chutneys. It is a cross between a traditional English marmalade and spicy Indian-style chutney. It is a little time consuming to make, but well worth the effort.

30 lemons, scrubbed well with soapy water and thoroughly rinsed

Salt to taste

2 cups raisins

1 cup white wine vinegar

2 cups brown sugar plus more if needed (optional)

4 Thai bird chilies or 2 tablespoons red pepper flakes

¼ cup coriander seeds, toasted and roughly crushed

Zest the lemons with a vegetable peeler. Cut the lemon zest into narrow strips, making sure to remove as much of the white pith as possible. Salt the zest well, and allow it to cure overnight. Cut the lemon flesh into segments, remove the bitter pith, and reserve.

The following day combine the zest, raisins, vinegar, brown sugar, and chilies in a heavy-bottomed saucepan. Bring to a boil over high heat, then lower the heat, and simmer until all the liquid has evaporated (it should take about 30 minutes). Fold in the lemon segments and coriander seeds, raise the heat to high, and cook for another 10 minutes, or until the lemon segments are tender, adding ¼ cup of water at a time, as necessary; the vinegar will keep evaporating. Taste for seasoning; the chutney may need more brown sugar depending

on the tartness of the lemons. Let
cool, then refrigerate. The chutney
will keep, refrigerated, for 6 months.

Options

➤ Try using limes, oranges, or
   grapefruit, or even a combination of citrus fruits.

➤ This chutney is delicious with
   cold meats, like chicken or lamb.

➤ Puree some chutney with a little
   oil for a quick marinade for lamb
   kebabs.

➤ Try putting some chutney in a
   sandwich or a wrap.

➤ Serve with cheeses and cold
   cuts for antipasto.

Fig and Cardamom Chutney

There is a natural affinity between cardamom and dried fruit. The floral sweetness of the cardamom offers a great counterpoint to the slightly dense, molasseslike flavor of dried fruit such as figs.

Makes 3 cups

25 dried figs, tough stems removed,
  cut into quarters (see Options
  below)
1 cup Madeira wine
1 cup water
1 onion, peeled and diced
1 apple, peeled and diced (see
  Options below)
1 teaspoon diced peeled fresh ginger
2 tablespoons ground cardamom
1 cup red wine vinegar
1 cup brown sugar

In 2-quart saucepan, simmer the figs, Madeira, and water together until the figs are tender and all the liquid has evaporated. Remove the figs to a medium bowl and set aside.

In the same pot over medium heat, caramelize the onion and apples. When the apples are tender and almost falling apart, add the remaining ingredients and return the figs to the saucepan. Reduce the heat and simmer until the mixture thickens. Let cool, then refrigerate.

Options

➤ If figs are in season, I like to fold a dozen or so stemmed and halved fresh figs into the mixture just before I use it, to brighten the flavors.

➤ I like using a tart apple like Granny Smith.

➤ This chutney is great with grilled lamb or chicken.

➤ I sometimes serve it with a cheese or rich Pork Rillettes (page 124).

➤ Pureed chutney makes a tasty sandwich spread, especially with a salty meat like prosciutto or country ham.

Green Mango Salad (page 4)

Grilled Asparagus Salad with Poached Egg and Shaved Parmesan (page 10)

Roasted Golden and Red Beet Salad with Goat Cheese Vinaigrette and Toasted Hazelnuts (page 15)

Rice Noodle Salad (page 22)

Green Chili Spoon Bread (page 37)

Preserved Lemons (page 62)

Red Pepper Marmalade (page 68)

Easy Red Duck Curry (page 102)

Braised Lamb Shanks (page 112)

Grilled Plum-Glazed Pork Belly (page 123)

Korean Beef and Rice Pot (page 125)

Cured Salmon Club Sandwich on Brioche with Chipotle Puree (page 140)

Steamed Mussels with Green Curry Broth (page 144)

Linguini with Roasted Cauliflower, Bacon, and Pine Nuts (page 158)

Grilled Pineapple and Vanilla Ice Cream (page 168)

Crème Brûlée with Orange Zesty Ice Cream (pages 172–173)

Quick Napa Cabbage Kimchi

Kimchi is a pickle or preserve that is a staple of the Korean kitchen. Think of it as spicy Asian sauerkraut. It is actually made the same way that sauerkraut is, with the addition of lots of red chili flakes and garlic. Kimchi is usually served as a side dish with boiled rice. For a while, we even made a daikon kimchi, but Pino Matteo, my chef de cuisine, detested the smell so much that it was banned from our kitchen. When you're making dishes that need to be fermented, make sure your work surfaces, mixing bowls, and containers are spotlessly clean. This recipe makes nearly a gallon of kimchi, but it will keep almost indefinitely tightly covered in the refrigerator.

Makes about 1 gallon

4 pounds napa cabbage

¾ cup kosher salt

2 cups water

1 cup red pepper flakes

2 tablespoons sugar

5 cloves garlic, chopped

**1 cup chopped onion, pureed in a
   miniprocessor**

Cut the cabbage into 1-inch pieces. Place in a very clean noncorrosive container (it can be a large plastic tub or a stainless steel pot). Dissolve the salt in the water, and pour it over the cabbage. Using your hands, mix well. Allow the mixture to sit for up to half a day at room temperature, tossing it from time to time. After 5 to 6 hours discard the liquid that has leached out of the cabbage.

Toss the cabbage with the remaining ingredients, and pack tightly into a container. Cover the surface with plastic wrap and weight it down (at the restaurant we fill a clean garbage bag with water and use it to weigh the cabbage down). Keep in a warm place for 24 hours. Transfer into smaller airtight jars and refrigerate.

Salsa Verde

This versatile salsa fits in all sorts of places. Try it over steamed fish fillets, on pork chops, in a falafel sandwich—even on a burger.

Makes about 3 cups

1 clove garlic

1 anchovy fillet

½ cup chopped parsley

½ cup chopped chives

½ cup minced tarragon leaves

½ cup minced dill leaves

½ cup minced chervil leaves

2 cups extra-virgin olive oil

**Salt and freshly ground black pepper
    to taste**

Mash the garlic and anchovy with a pestle in a mortar. Blend with the remaining ingredients. Correct seasoning if necessary.

Chunky Peanut-Tamarind Sauce

In Malaysia, this sauce is known as satay sauce because it is usually served with satay (skewered cubes of meat, fish, or poultry); in Indonesia, it is served with *gado gado* (an Indonesian version of salad niçoise). Try it! It's surprisingly versatile and even good enough to eat on its own. *Sambal*—basically a heady mixture of chilies, brown sugar, and salt—is available at Malaysian and some Chinese markets (see Ingredient Sources, page 199).

Makes over 3 cups

2 shallots, diced

1 clove garlic, roughly chopped

1 cup smooth peanut butter

1 cup tamarind paste

¼ cup *sambal*

¼ cup vinegar

¼ cup sugar

Water as needed

Salt to taste

1 cup toasted peanuts, roughly
   chopped

In a heavy-bottomed saucepan, sweat the shallots and garlic over medium-low heat until soft, about 5 minutes. Add the remaining ingredients except the chopped nuts. Cook over low heat for 15 minutes or until the sauce reaches the consistency you like. You can vary this further by adjusting the amount of water you add. Finally, fold in the toasted nuts. This sauce will thicken as it sits. Let cool, and refrigerate. The sauce will keep, tightly covered and refrigerated, for a week.

Options

➤ Serve the sauce as a dip for crudités.

➤ Serve with satay (my favorite recipe is on page 202 of *Cooking from A to Z*).

➤ Toss with julienned carrots, cucumbers, and egg noodles for a quick and simple chinese noodle salad.

➤ Serve as a sauce for Shrimp and Julienned Vegetable–Filled Tofu (page 46).

Gingered Pineapple Glaze

Back when we first opened AZ, I really wanted to put Buffalo wings on our lounge menu, but they did seem a little lowbrow, so I developed this recipe. The predominant flavors in Buffalo wings are spice and acid. This glaze produces similar flavors, but it's a little rounder and fruitier because of the pineapple juice.

Makes 1 cup

4 cups pineapple juice (canned is fine)

1 cup brown sugar

2 cups chopped or crushed ginger

2 habeñero chile peppers

1 cup champagne vinegar

Bring all the ingredients to a boil over high heat in a heavy-bottomed skillet. Lower the heat and simmer until the liquid has reduced by three-quarters. Puree and strain.

Options

➤ Brush the glaze on ham while baking.

➤ Make a zesty pork chop marinade by adding a little oil to the glaze.

➤ Or make Buffalo wings: Dredge the trimmed wings in seasoned flour, deep-fry, then toss the hot wings with the glaze.

➤ Try tossing grilled pineapple chunks with the glaze and serving it with vanilla ice cream.

Orange-Scented Hoisin Sauce

Hoisin is a Chinese bean paste sauce that can be found in any Asian market as well as in most larger supermarkets. It is almost like the mayonnaise of Chinese cooking. It can be used out of the jar, but I like brightening it up with other flavors to make it special.

Makes about 1 quart

2 cups hoisin sauce

2 cups freshly squeezed orange
   juice, from about 6 to 8 oranges

Grated zest of 2 oranges

A pinch of finely ground cumin seeds

¼ cup lemon oil (optional)

Reduce the orange juice by half. Fold in all the other ingredients. Will keep, tightly covered and refrigerated, for up to a month.

Chicken and Poultry

Chicken is affordable and incredibly versatile; duck, quail, and turkey vary the poultry diet considerably. Above all, in this section I've tried to make chicken and poultry exciting again with some unusual and highly flavorful recipes.

Parchment-Wrapped Chicken Scented with Ginger and Five-Spice Powder

This dish will appeal to even the fussiest eater in your family. I speak from experience; when I was a child I was such a picky eater that this was the only food I would eat when I visited my family in Malaysia. Not only is it delicious, it is quite a lot of fun unwrapping a fried parchment paper–wrapped parcel. If you don't want to bother wrapping the chicken, just roast it in a shallow roasting pan, but the chicken is never as flavorful or as moist. This is a great dish to bring to picnics.

Makes 8 servings

¼ cup soy sauce

2 tablespoons sugar

2 tablespoons diced ginger

1 tablespoon Basic Five-Spice
   Powder (page 52)

8 scallions, white parts only, cut into
   2-inch lengths

4 chicken breast halves, skinned

4 chicken thighs, boned and skinned

8 pieces parchment paper,
   approximately 10 by 5 inches

Peanut oil for deep frying

In a large bowl, combine the soy sauce, sugar, ginger, five-spice powder, and scallions. Whisk until the ingredients are well combined. Turn the chicken pieces in the mixture to coat them, and marinate, covered and refrigerated, for up to 12 hours but no less than an hour.

Place a parchment-paper piece on a work surface, with the 10-inch sides at the top and bottom. Put a piece of chicken and one to two scallion pieces in the center of the paper. Fold the top half of the paper down over the chicken to meet the bottom of the paper. Fold up the open edges to form a fairly tight seal. Repeat with all the chicken and parchment, to make eight tightly sealed packets.

Heat an inch of the oil over high heat in a deep-sided pot, 15 minutes before serving. When the oil reaches 350 degrees, lower the heat and fry three to five packets at a time, slipping them slowly and carefully into the oil. Turn the packets over a few times with long tongs, and fry for 7 to 10 minutes. Drain and serve the chicken in the packets.

Options

➢ The chicken can be baked (with or without the packet) in a 400-degree oven for 15 minutes.

➢ I usually serve it with plain steamed rice and a nice tangy cucumber salad.

➢ Another option is to serve the chicken at room temperature with a pasta salad. This is especially good for picnics or really hot days when you don't want to cook for very long.

Roasted Five-Spice Chicken

This may seem like a long recipe, especially the preparation and butchering of the chicken, but it is well worth the time. Or you could save time and ask your butcher to bone the chicken for you.

Makes 2 generous servings

2 small chickens, about 2 to 3 pounds each

½ cup (1 stick) unsalted butter, softened

2 tablespoons Basic Five-Spice Powder (page 52)

1 tablespoon chopped fresh tarragon leaves

Juice and grated zest of 1 lemon

Salt and freshly ground black pepper to taste

2 tablespoons canola oil

Remove the backbone, ribs, and thigh bones from the chicken: Cut along both sides of the backbone with a pair of poultry shears. Once you have removed the backbone and attached tail, the ribs, the sternum, and hip bones should rip out quite easily in such a small chicken. With a sharp paring knife, cut each thigh with two lengthwise slashes to expose the thigh bones. Cut around each bone to free it of meat. Holding the tip of the bone in one hand, scrape the meat from the bone. Twist the bone at the "knee" joint to detach it. Reserve the bones for stock.

With a fork, mix the butter with the five-spice powder, lemon juice and zest, and tarragon. If the butter seems too soft after the other ingredients are incorporated, refrigerate it briefly.

With your fingers, gently separate the skin from the breast of the chicken, and slip some compound butter under the skin. Season the birds all over with salt and pepper. Pat the chicken dry with paper towels.

Preheat the oven to 350 degrees.

Add the oil to a cast-iron sauté pan or heavy skillet over medium-high heat. Allow the oil to heat for 2 to 3 minutes, then carefully place the chicken, skin side down, in the pan. Reduce the heat to low. Place a second heavy skillet on top of the chicken to press it into the pan. Allow the chicken to brown, undisturbed, for 10 to 15 minutes. When the skin is golden brown, remove the second skillet from the chicken and transfer the pan to the oven for another 10 to 15 minutes. Serve at once.

Options

➤ Serve the chicken with steamed rice and stir-fried vegetables.

➤ Pick the meat off the chicken, toss with a little mayonnaise, use for sandwich filling or in a wrap.

➤ Serve the chicken with Green Chili Spoon Bread (page 37) or a quick fried rice.

Cornflake-Crusted Chicken Breast

A variation of this dish was on the menu at Miracle Grill, where I first started working with Bobby Flay. (I started as the salad wench.) It is essentially fried chicken with more robust flavors and a really crunchy crust. I use a chicken breast because that is how I've done it in my restaurants, but you can use easier-to-eat drumsticks if you are making this for a picnic, or cut the breast into strips for a child's meal. A French-cut chicken breast is a breast with the first joint of the wing still attached.

Makes 2 servings

2 skinless French-cut chicken breast
   halves
Salt and freshly ground black pepper
   to taste
1 cup all-purpose flour
1 cup Red Pepper Marmalade
   (page 68)
4 cups cornflakes, crushed in a pie
   plate
¼ cup canola oil
2 tablespoons butter

Rinse the breasts well in cold water, pat them dry, and season with salt and pepper. Dredge each breast lightly in flour, then generously smear the Red Pepper Marmalade over each breast. I find this easiest to do with my hands; it's a little messy, but you get the best results. Dredge the breasts in the cornflakes, pressing to make sure that all the chicken surfaces are covered.

Preheat the oven to 350 degrees.

Add the oil to a large cast-iron pan or a heavy sauté pan over high heat. Allow the oil to heat for about 3 to 4 minutes, then carefully add the chicken breasts. Lower the heat to medium, and fry for 3 to 4 minutes until golden brown. Turn the breasts and cook for another 2 minutes. Add the butter to the skillet and transfer it to the oven for another 2 minutes. Serve immediately with creamy pureed Yukon gold potatoes and crunchy green beans.

Options

➣ Instead of crushed cornflakes, dredge the chicken in bread crumbs, cornmeal, *panko*, or crushed wheat flakes—even instant mashed potato flakes—before frying.

➣ This is another dish that is just as good at room temperature; serve with a green salad and a spicy, tangy Corn Salsa (page 60).

Curried Grilled Chicken with Lemongrass, Ginger, and Macadamia Nuts

Kelantan is a Malaysian state that borders southern Thailand. This grilled chicken uses some flavors that are prevalent there. It's a great hit at cookouts. It's also a nice change from the usual tomato-based barbecue sauce. I like using dark meat when I barbecue because, in order for the meat to develop a smoky flavor and for the glaze to caramelize, the heat has to be quite high, which would dry out white meat. The chicken needs to marinate overnight, so plan accordingly.

Makes 4 servings

4 chicken drumsticks

4 chicken thighs

1 tablespoon Madras curry powder (use your favorite variety)

1 tablespoon ancho chili powder (available in Mexican or Hispanic markets, and many gourmet food shops)

2 teaspoons ground turmeric powder

1 tablespoon sugar

Salt to taste

1 cup finely chopped lemongrass

4 cloves garlic, finely chopped

1 (1-inch) piece galangal (Southeast Asian ginger; see Options below)

½ cup toasted macadamia nuts

2 jalapeño peppers, roughly chopped (remove the seeds and ribs if you want a milder result)

½ cup tamarind pulp

½ cup unsweetened coconut milk

2 tablespoons dark brown sugar or palm sugar

Prick the chicken all over with the tines of a fork then place in a large nonreactive bowl. Add the curry powder, chili powder, turmeric, and sugar and allow to marinate refrigerated overnight.

Place the remaining ingredients in the workbowl of a food processor and pulse until the mixture forms a puree. Grill the chicken over high heat, basting constantly with the macadamia and coconut milk puree. Serve hot or chilled with a crisp green salad and pickled cucumber.

Options

➢ If you substitute regular ginger, use half the amount and add the grated zest of 1 lemon.

➢ This chicken is great served cold.

➢ Shred the meat to toss with a crunchy romaine salad with buttermilk dressing.

➢ Mix the shredded meat with a little mayonnaise for a delicious sandwich filling.

Spicy Fried Chicken

I have never met anyone who does not like fried chicken. This recipe is a cross between tandoori chicken and fried chicken. The chicken is marinated for at least 6 hours (overnight is better) in spiced yogurt, then dredged in cornmeal, then fried. Serve the fried chicken with coleslaw and potato salad.

I like to cut the chicken up into "fingers" because it's easier to eat that way. But when I make this dish at home, I like to keep the chicken on the bone. It's more fun to eat, and I think it keeps the meat a lot more moist and flavorful.

Makes enough for 3 to 4 servings

2 tablespoons Garam Masala (page 55)

1 tablespoon ground turmeric

2 tablespoons finely chopped garlic

¼ cup finely chopped ginger

1 large chicken, cut into 10 pieces, about 4 pounds (the wings, drumsticks, thighs, and 2 pieces out of each breasts)

1 quart yogurt

2 quarts yellow or white cornmeal or instant polenta

Salt and freshly ground black pepper to taste

6 cups canola oil, or Crisco or lard if you want really crispy chicken

Stir the Garam Masala, turmeric, garlic, and ginger into the yogurt. Place the chicken in a large bowl or sealable plastic bag and pour the yogurt over the chicken. Cover tightly or seal the bag, and refrigerate for 6 to 8 hours or overnight.

Dredge the chicken in cornmeal seasoned with salt and pepper. In a Dutch oven or a large pot (I use a wok at home), heat the canola oil. If you do not have an oil thermometer you can determine whether the oil is hot enough by tossing in a small piece of white bread. If it browns rapidly, the oil is hot enough. Reduce the heat to medium and carefully add the chicken piece by piece, making sure that the oil does not bubble over.

If you find that the chicken is brown enough on the exterior, but is not cooked in the center, cover with foil and put it into a preheated 350-degree oven.

Serve with wedges of lemon.

Hunter's Chicken

Like most people I have a pantry filled with small quantities of ingredients—never enough for a recipe, but too much to throw away. I named this dish Hunter's Chicken not because it bears any relation to French Hunter's Chicken *(Poulet Chasseur),* but because I generally hunt around in my pantry for the odds and ends to use in the stew. A few dried porcini mushrooms, four pieces of dried shiitake, the odd carrot and celery stalk in the refrigerator, an onion or two, a stray bay leaf, and you have a simple but delicious one-pot dish. I like to keep the chicken on the bone for this recipe as it makes the stew richer and more rustic. You can make this with any type of meat; I happen to like chicken. Use the ingredients in this recipe as just a guideline for your own pantry hunting and improvisations.

Make 4 to 6 servings

1 (5-pound) chicken, cut into 10 to
    12 pieces

2 cups flour, well seasoned with
    Spanish paprika, salt, and freshly
    ground black pepper

2 tablespoons canola oil

½ pound Chinese sausage, cut into
    1-inch pieces

2 carrots, peeled and cut into bite-
    sized chunks

2 stalks celery, cut into bite-sized
    chunks

2 onions, cut into 2-inch pieces

20 small white button mushrooms

1 ounce dried porcini mushrooms,
    rehydrated in ½ cup warm
    water

8 dried shiitake mushroom caps,
    rehydrated in 1 cup hot water

2 tablespoons tomato puree

1 cup dry red wine

1 cup chicken stock

1 cup pearl barley

2 bay leaves

1 tablespoon fresh thyme leaves

Wash the chicken, pat dry, and dredge in seasoned flour. Add the oil to a large Dutch oven or heavy-bottomed pot over high heat. Brown the chicken pieces without crowding, in batches as necessary. Remove the pieces as they brown. Set aside.

Drain most of the oil from the pan and return the pot to medium-high heat. Add the Chinese sausage, carrots, celery, onions, and button mushrooms. Cook, stirring often, for 7 to 8 minutes, or until the vegetables are caramelized. I like to cook the vegetables until they are mahogany-colored, which takes at least another 5 minutes.

While the vegetables are cooking, roughly chop the rehydrated porcini and shiitake mushrooms. Strain and reserve the soaking liquids.

Add the tomato puree to the vegetables and cook, stirring, for another minute or two. Return the chicken to the pot with the chopped mushrooms. Cover with the mushroom liquid, wine, and chicken stock. Bring to a boil over high heat, then reduce the heat to medium. Stir in the pearl barley and herbs. Simmer, covered, for 35 to 45 minutes. Discard the bay leaves before serving.

Serve with pureed potatoes or thick slices of grilled sourdough bread to soak up the juices.

Easy Red Duck Curry

This is a recipe for those of us who are both lazy and busy. Your guests will think you have slaved for hours over this dish. I am a great believer in shopping well. Chinese barbecued duck can be found in most Chinatown shops, where they will usually chop it up for you. Or just pick up a roasted chicken at your supermarket, or use roasted pork instead.

Makes 3 to 4 servings

1 can unsweetened coconut milk, unshaken

1 tablespoon red curry paste

2 tablespoons Thai fish sauce

1 tablespoon brown sugar

2 cans coconut milk

1 stalk lemongrass, smashed

2 kaffir lime leaves, finely chopped

Juice of 2 limes

1 (4- to 5-pound) barbecued duck, cut into 10 pieces

Remove the top layer of cream from an unshaken can of coconut milk, and place it in a sauté pan over low heat, stirring frequently until the cream starts to separate. Add the curry paste, fish sauce, and brown sugar. Stir for 5 minutes or until the mixture darkens slightly. Add the coconut milk, lemongrass, and kaffir lime leaves and simmer for 10 minutes; add the lime juice and barbecued duck pieces. Heat through. Serve over steamed rice.

Options

➢ I like adding diced pineapple to the dish.

➢ For a vegetarian version, add grilled or roasted eggplant, diced firm tofu, and baby bok choy.

Roasted Duck and Wild Rice Salad

The nutty flavor and texture of the wild rice marries really well with the rich and slightly gamy flavor of good roasted duck. I don't usually roast a whole duck just for this dish. Your best bet is to buy a roasted duck from your nearest Chinatown. Or you could buy 1 large or 2 medium duck breast halves, dice the meat, and sear it yourself.

Makes 4 servings

1 cup diced roasted duck

2 cups cooked wild rice

1 Granny Smith apple, diced

1 small cucumber, seeded and diced

2 stalks celery, diced

2 oranges, cut into segments

½ cup soy sauce

¼ cup freshly squeezed lime juice

1 tablespoon *sambal* (Indonesian
   seasoning, available in most
   Asian markets)

1 tablespoon sugar

1 tablespoon toasted sesame oil

1 bunch watercress, roughly chopped

Toss all the ingredients together except the watercress. Add the cress just before serving.

Option

➤ This recipe also works well with chicken, preferably dark meat.

Duck Liver and Bacon Roll
with Honey-Hoisin Glaze

This dish is the Cantonese version of rumaki (chicken livers and water chestnuts wrapped in bacon, then broiled). I use a lot of duck in my restaurants, so there is always a great deal of duck liver available. Even people who think they don't like liver will like this.

Makes 6

6 large pieces duck liver

Flour for dusting

**Salt and freshly ground black pepper
   to taste**

2 tablespoons canola oil

6 strips bacon

**6 trimmed scallions, cut into 2-inch
   lengths**

**6 strips carrots, about ¼ inch thick,
   2 inches long**

**6 strips stemmed, seeded jalapeño
   pepper, 2 inches long**

3 tablespoons honey

¼ cup hoisin sauce

2 tablespoons rice wine vinegar

Preheat the broiler.

Clean the livers well, cutting off any discolored areas and removing any veins or fat. Pat them dry and dust them lightly with the flour seasoned with salt and pepper and sauté in the canola oil in a hot pan for 1 minute on each side. Remove.

Lay the bacon strips on a cookie sheet and broil for 1 minute until some of the fat has rendered out and it is half cooked. Once the bacon is cool enough to handle, lay it on a flat surface. Place a piece each of liver, scallion, carrot, and jalapeño on one end and roll up. Secure with a toothpick or a skewer. Repeat with the remaining ingredients.

Lightly toss each bacon roll in the honey, hoisin, and rice wine vinegar. Place on a cookie sheet and broil for a minute on each side or until the glaze turns a deep mahogany. Serve immediately.

Tandoori Grilled Quail

A tandoor is an Indian clay oven. Like most wood-burning ovens, a tandoor gets really hot. Unfortunately, most of us do not have a tandoor. In this recipe, I use the traditional spices used in tandoori and, rather than cooking the quail in an oven, I cook them on a grill. If you are unable to find quail, try using chicken or a game hen instead.

Makes 2 servings

1 cup whole-milk yogurt

1 tablespoon Garam Masala (page 55)

1 tablespoon sweet paprika (I prefer Spanish smoked paprika)

1 tablespoon cayenne

¼ cup finely chopped mint

Juice and grated zest of 1 lime

4 quail, partially boned and butterflied

Stir the yogurt, Garam Masala, paprika, cayenne, mint, and lime juice and zest together in a glass measure. Place the quail in a sealable plastic bag, pour the marinade over the quail, press the air pockets out of the bag, and seal it. Marinate the quail for up to 1 day.

Grill the quail on a hot grill for 10 minutes on the skin side and another 5 minutes on the other side. Serve with a small salad tossed in Maple Vinaigrette (page 64).

Option

➤ Try using shrimp or lobster instead of the quails, but marinate only up to 1 hour, or else the yogurt will start to denature the protein, making the shellfish mushy.

Meat

There are times when I crave a big juicy steak. But most of the time, my favorite meat meals are flavorful stews, cooked slowly so the meat creates its own sauce. The slow cooking also allows flavors to develop and marry, your home smells great, and although it may appear as if you have been toiling for hours over your stove, such dishes can actually be quite simple.

I love braising meats in the cooler months of the year, but come summer all I want to do is grill. There is something about cooking and eating outdoors that is so festive, bug bites and all. If you don't have a grill or can't grill outdoors, most of these recipes can be accomplished using a grill pan on your stove top, or with an electric grill.

Thai Pork Curry

The first time I tasted a Masaman curry, I was visiting the family of my friend O in Nakhon Si Thammarat in southwestern Thailand. My traveling companions and I spoke no Thai, and O's family spoke no English, yet we still had a wonderful day together, especially because they were so willing to share their home, their kitchen, and this recipe. Masaman curry is a southern Thai curry, strongly influenced by Indian spices. Unlike the curries from the north, which contain lemongrass, kaffir lime, and coriander, southern Thai curries are redolent with sweet spices and chilies, but because it's Thai, it's also sparked with the citric flavors of lemongrass and limes. If you don't want to use pork, try this with chicken or beef.

Makes 4 main course portions

1 tablespoon coriander seeds

1 tablespoon cumin seeds

1 tablespoon black peppercorns

1 tablespoon fennel

¼ cup canola oil

2 pounds pork butt (shoulder), cut into 2-inch cubes

2 onions, diced

5 cloves garlic, peeled and finely chopped

1 carrot, roughly chopped

¼ cup diced fresh ginger

1 tablespoon ground turmeric powder

3 jalapeño peppers, seeds and ribs removed, diced

4 roasted red bell peppers, steamed in a plastic bag for 15 minutes, skin rubbed off with paper towels, roughly chopped

1 tablespoon red chili flakes (optional—add it if you like your curries hot)

2 cups beef or chicken stock or water

2 lemongrass stalks, trimmed and smashed but still intact

1 (13- to 14-ounce) can coconut cream

Grated zest and juice of 4 limes

Kosher salt to taste

¼ cup chopped cilantro leaves

¼ cup chopped mint leaves

In a large dry skillet, toast the coriander, cumin, peppercorns, and fennel over medium heat for 4 minutes, shaking constantly. Let the mixture cool slightly, then grind finely in a spice grinder and set aside.

Place the same skillet over high heat and add 2 tablespoons of the canola oil. Brown the pork in batches without overcrowding the skillet. Remove each batch to a large plate. Set aside. Lower the heat to medium and add the remaining oil and the onions, garlic, and carrot. Cook until the vegetables are tender, about 10 minutes.

Raise the heat to high again, and add the reserved ground spice mixture, ginger, turmeric, jalapeños, peppers, and optional red chili flakes. Sauté for 5 minutes, stirring until really fragrant. Add the reserved pork, stock, and lemongrass. Bring to just a simmer over medium heat, then reduce the heat to a simmer and cook for 40 minutes. Stir in the coconut cream. Season with the lime zest and juice and the salt. Just before serving, fish out the lemongrass stalk, and fold in the chopped cilantro and mint. Serve with steamed rice or Coconut Rice Croquettes (page 162) and Green Mango Salad (page 4).

Pork Tonkatsu

The duck schnitzel I served at AZ (the recipe is in my *Cooking from A to Z*) is based on a Japanese cutlet called *tonkatsu*. Italians do a version in veal called a veal Milanese, which is also quite similar. This is my variation with pork, in a cut easy to find at any supermarket.

Makes 4 servings

4 boneless pork loin chops, ¾ inch thick

Salt and freshly ground black pepper to taste

2 large eggs, beaten

¼ cup freshly grated Parmigiano-Reggiano cheese

2 cups *panko* (Japanese bread crumbs) or your favorite dried unflavored bread crumbs

4 tablespoons canola oil

½ cup (1 stick) unsalted butter

Preheat the oven to 200 degrees.

Place the pork chops between two sheets of waxed paper, and with a mallet or the bottom of a heavy sauté pan, pound the chop until it is about ⅛ of an inch thick. Repeat until all four chops are done. Season with salt and pepper.

In a pie plate or large flat bowl, mix the eggs with the cheese. Put the bread crumbs in another bowl. Dredge each chop in the egg mixture, then press both sides of the chop into the bread crumbs. Repeat until all four chops are finished.

In a large sauté pan over high heat, heat the canola oil for 2 minutes or until hot. Carefully place a chop in the hot oil. (Do not overcrowd the pan or the chops will steam rather than form a crisp crust. Do them one at a time if necessary.) Reduce the heat to medium, sauté the chop for 3 minutes or until golden, and for the last minute add about a quarter of the butter. Turn and continue cooking for another minute. Remove the chop to an ovenproof dish and place in the preheated oven to keep warm while you cook the other chops. Wipe the oil, butter, and burned bread crumb bits out of the skillet before proceeding with each chop.

Options

➢ Serve the cutlets with a salad of watercress, finely sliced cabbage, and julienned apples for a light lunch or supper.

➢ Sandwich the pork between focaccia slices with green olive tapanade and mayonnaise for a delicious treat.

➢ Try using chicken or turkey breasts, or veal scallops, instead of pork.

Braised Lamb Shanks

Whenever I braise lamb shanks, I make enough for at least two meals. Like most braised meat dishes, the flavors get better as the stew sits.

Makes 6 ample servings

6 lamb shanks, about 1 pound each

2 tablespoons canola oil

1 onion, diced

2 carrots, peeled and diced

2 stalks celery, cut into chunks

2 cups canned diced tomatoes, with their juice

1 cup full-bodied red wine

10 to 15 sprigs thyme

¼ cup dried porcini mushrooms, soaked in warm water for 15 minutes, drained, and roughly chopped

2 cups cooked white beans

Preheat the oven to 300 degrees.

Brown the lamb shanks in the canola oil in a large ovenproof pot with a lid over medium-high heat, in batches, if necessary, to avoid crowding. Remove the shanks and place the vegetables in the same pot, stirring every 3 to 4 minutes until caramelized. Return all the lamb shanks to the pot with the tomatoes, red wine, thyme sprigs, and porcini mushrooms, and bring everything to just a simmer.

Cover the pot, put it into the pre-heated oven, and cook slowly for 2½ to 3 hours. During the final half hour of cooking, remove the lid, add the white beans, and finish braising.

Options

➤ Serve the shanks with mashed potatoes, Smoky Tomato Polenta (page 156) or Wild Mushroom Risotto (page 160).

➤ Try dusting the lamb shanks with the Indian spice blend Garam Masala (page 55) before browning.

➤ Leave out the white beans; substitute cauliflower and okra for the last half hour of cooking.

➤ I sometimes make a Mint Pesto (page 59) to serve with the shanks.

➤ Pick the meat off the shanks, toss with pasta and soft goat cheese.

➤ You could also serve the shredded meat with couscous.

Spicy Lamb Sausage

Spicy lamb sausage is also known as *merguez*, and it is also made with beef, but never pork. It's a popular snack in Morocco and other parts of North Africa. At home I make the sausage into patties, but if you want to stuff the meat into casing, be sure to let the meat rest and cure in the refrigerator for a day or two.

Makes 3 to 4 servings

1 pound ground lamb (from a leg or shoulder cut, including as much fat as possible)

4 cloves garlic

1 tablespoon cayenne

2 tablespoons Aleppo chili powder

2 tablespoons toasted ground coriander seeds

2 tablespoons toasted ground cumin seeds

1 tablespoon dried thyme

Mix all the ingredients together with your hands. Make into patties, and allow to cure wrapped in parchment for at least 1 day.

Options

➤ Grill the sausage patties and stuff them into pita pockets with a raita (recipe follows).

➤ Serve sausage on couscous with lots of fresh herbs and some toasted pistachios.

Raita

Makes 4 servings

**2 medium cucumbers, about
   1½ pounds**

1½ cups plain whole-milk yogurt

½ cup sour cream

**½ teaspoon toasted cumin seeds,
   ground**

½ teaspoon kosher salt

2 tablespoons minced cilantro leaves

Peel, halve, and seed the cucumbers. Grate them into a bowl using the large holes of a box grater. Add the yogurt, sour cream, cumin, salt, and cilantro, and mix well. Serve thoroughly chilled.

Stir-Fried Beef with Black Beans

Stir-frying is such a quick and easy cooking method—the only time-consuming aspect is the initial prep work. The meat and vegetables have to be cut into bite-sized pieces so that everything will cook quickly over high heat. This recipe calls for hanger steak, which is a relatively inexpensive, deeply flavored, and slightly tough cut of meat.

Makes 3 to 4 servings

1 pound hanger steak

2 tablespoons fermented black beans

¼ cup julienned ginger

2 cloves garlic, chopped

4 tablespoons canola oil

1 bunch scallions, white and pale green parts only, cut into 1-inch lengths

1 red bell pepper, julienned

2 jalapeño peppers, sliced crosswise into rings

5 shiitake mushroom caps, julienned

¼ cup beef stock

2 tablespoons miso

Cut the hanger steak against the grain into strips.

Soak the fermented black beans in warm water for 10 minutes. Drain the beans, and puree them in a miniprocessor with the ginger and garlic. Pulse in 1 tablespoon of the canola oil, then massage the puree into the steak. Set the steak aside to marinate while you prep the vegetables.

In a wok over really high heat, add 2 tablespoons of the canola oil. Quickly stir-fry the beef for 3 minutes, and remove it from the pan. Add the last tablespoon of oil and stir-fry the scallions, peppers, and mushrooms for 3 minutes. Return the beef to the wok with the stock and miso. Stir for 1 minute and serve.

Options

➤ Serve this stir-fry with orange hoisin sauce as a filling for a lettuce wrap. If you are unable to find a moo shu wrap you like, consider making a simple crêpe or even using flour tortillas.

➤ Serve this simple stir-fry over fresh rice noodles. Blanch the noodles, then toss them with scallions and chili oil and top with the stir-fry.

➤ Add some baby bok choy or broccoli to the stir-fry and serve over rice.

Pork Vindaloo

Vindaloo is a dish from Kerala, which is located on the southwestern coast of India. This vinegary and spicy dish reflects the Portuguese influences in the cuisine of this region; the area was colonized and ruled by the Portuguese for over two hundred years. Vindaloos are popular in Malaysia as well because it, too, was once a Portuguese colony and because of the large Indian population of the country.

In this dish, I try to use pork shoulder, which has more flavor and can handle the long braising better than leaner cuts.

Makes 6 servings

¼ cup canola oil

1 cup flour

2 tablespoons Garam Masala
    (page 55)

2 pounds pork shoulder, cut into
    2-inch cubes

1 cup peeled diced fresh ginger

2 large onions, finely diced

4 cloves garlic

1 tablespoon ground toasted
    coriander seeds

1 tablespoon ground toasted
    cardamom pods

1 tablespoon ground toasted cumin
    seeds

1 tablespoon ground toasted fennel
    seeds

1 tablespoon green peppercorns

5 green jalapeño peppers,
    stemmed and minced
    (See Options below)

1 cup cider vinegar

1 cup dry red wine

1 cup stock or water

2 cups diced tomatoes

25 okra, stemmed

Heat the canola oil in a heavy-bottomed pot over high heat. Mix the flour with the Garam Masala. Dust the pork with the seasoned flour and brown it, in batches, if necessary, to avoid crowding, about 10 minutes per batch. Remove browned meat and reserve.

Lower the heat to medium-high, and add ginger, onions, and garlic to the pot. Sauté until golden brown, then stir in the ground spices, peppercorns, and jalapeño peppers. Continue cooking for a further 5 minutes until it is really fragrant; return the pork to pot. Add the vinegar, wine, and stock, bring the mixture to a boil, then reduce the heat and simmer on medium for 25 minutes. Add the tomatoes and okra and continue cooking over medium heat for another 20 minutes or until the okra is just tender.

Note: Browning the meat is not traditional in making curries. Traditionally the aromatics are cooked, then the meat added at the same time as all the liquids. I like browning the meat because it gives the curry a more tawny color, and the flour helps thicken the sauce a little.

Options

➢ Use 2 poblanos instead, if you want a less spicy vindaloo.

➢ Try using chicken or lamb for this dish. A word of advice, though: I like using a tougher cut of meat because it is more flavorful. If you use a really lean cut of meat, just cook it for less time by removing the meat as soon as it's tender, and reduce the sauce to the consistency you like.

➢ You can also make this dish vegetarian by using eggplant, potatoes, and/or any vegetables you like.

➢ Okra is a delicious vegetable but much maligned because of its reputation for sliminess. I find that if you use really young pods they tend to be less slimy. The mucilaginous quality of the okra actually helps thicken the sauce.

Braised Ham Shanks

Ham shanks are a wonderful—and wonderfully inexpensive—cut of meat. It is a fairly tough cut, though, and does benefit from long, slow cooking.

Makes 4 servings

**4 large ham shanks, generally about
 1½ pounds**

**Salt and freshly ground black pepper
 to taste**

**1 (4-inch) piece peeled ginger, sliced
 into coins**

1 head garlic

1 (3-inch) stick cinnamon

3 star anise

1 small onion

2 cloves (stabbed into the onion)

1 tablespoon black peppercorns

2 cups soy sauce

2 cups sake

2 cups stock or water

2 cups Coca-Cola

Heat the oven to 350 degrees.

Place a pot large enough to hold all the shanks over medium-high heat. Season the shanks with salt and pepper, and brown them on all sides. Add the remaining ingredients, cover tightly with foil, and braise in the oven for 4 to 5 hours,

until the meat is falling off the bone. Cool in the braising liquid.

Remove the shanks from liquid, remove any excess fat, and if you don't like the texture of the skin, remove that, too.

Options

➤ Serve the shanks with steamed white rice and sugar snap peas that have been sautéed quickly in a touch of sesame oil.

➤ Shred the flesh off the bone, toss with rice noodles or your favorite noodles, shiitake mushrooms, and leafy greens.

➤ The shanks are also great served with Roasted Cauliflower (page 158).

Asian Egg Noodles with Pork

This is a stir-fry noodle dish that uses thick-cut egg noodles. You will find these in Asian markets labeled as either Hokkien Noodles or Shanghai-style egg noodles. I have used bucatini as a substitute.

Makes 4 servings

1 pound dried or fresh thick-cut egg noodles

Canola oil for frying

½ pound minced pork

2 scallions, green and white parts chopped into 2-inch lengths and kept separate

2 garlic cloves, finely chopped

2 jalapeño peppers, chopped

8 shiitake mushrooms, stemmed and quartered

½ cup sugar snap peas

3 tablespoons soy sauce

1 tablespoon *kecap manis* (sweet soybean sauce)

Juice of 1 lime

Cilantro leaves for garnish

Cook the noodles according to package instructions and set aside. In a wok, heat a little oil and stir-fry the pork over high heat until browned. Remove and keep warm.

Stir-fry the white parts of the scallions with the garlic and jalapeño in a little more oil until fragrant. Add the mushrooms and cook for 2 to 3 minutes, then return the pork to the pan. Add the cooked noodles, sugar snaps, and scallion greens with a little more oil, and stir-fry for a minute or two, allowing the sugar snaps to cook and the noodles to pick up a little smoky flavor. Finally, add the soy, *kecap manis*, and lime juice. Heat through. Remove from the heat and stir in the cilantro leaves.

Grilled Plum-Glazed Pork Belly

I really like pork belly, probably because I love bacon. This dish is quick to cook, but requires a little preparation time. Don't be put off by the apparent fattiness of the belly, because most of the fat will render off during the cooking process. You may have to order the belly ahead of time from your butcher, and also have him remove the rind. If you are like me, you'll save the rind to make fried pork crackling strips. They are delicious sprinkled over fried rice or pad thai. The fried pork cracklings also make a delicious bar snack.

Makes 4 to 6 servings

1 (2-pound) slab pork belly

1 tablespoon finely diced ginger

1 cup plum puree (or your favorite plum jam)

½ cup red wine vinegar

2 tablespoons *sambal* (Indonesian spice blend, available in most Asian markets)

Salt and freshly ground pepper to taste

Wrap the belly in plastic wrap and freeze it for a half hour to make it easier to handle. Cut the belly into ½-inch slices. Marinate the slices in a mixture of the ginger, plum puree, red wine vinegar, *sambal*, salt, and pepper for up to 2 hours. Grill over high heat. Or, if a grill isn't available, use a ridged grill pan over medium-high heat in a well-ventilated kitchen.

Options

➤ Serve over steamed rice or rice noodles.

➤ Cut the belly strips into smaller pieces and use in lettuce rolls with pickled onions and brandied hoisin sauce (recipe in my *Cooking from A to Z*).

➤ Wrap in rice paper with cilantro, basil, and mint. Serve with Thai fish sauce.

Pork Rillettes

Whenever I butcher pork, I have a lot of trimmings left over and I hate throwing them away. An Asian kitchen is thrifty and makes use of everything. I make a confit with the meat, using a mixture of pork and duck fat. If I run out of duck fat in the restaurant I sometimes use a mild cooking oil like canola oil. The pork confit is delicious diced into pieces and thrown into stir-fry or made into this great rillette. Rillette is a potted meat spread, and although the combination of ingredients in this recipe sounds a little strange it is perfectly delicious.

Makes about 2 cups

1 pound pork (try not to use really lean cuts for this)

For the Curing Mix

1 part salt, ½ part sugar, and your favorite dried herbs to taste

4 cups canola oil

½ cup crème fraîche

½ cup dried apricots, diced with a knife dipped in canola oil

½ cup toasted pistachios, lightly chopped

Preheat the oven to 300 degrees.

Cure the pork in the curing mix overnight. Then rinse off the cure, pat the meat dry, and put it in an ovenproof pot or dish. Pour the canola oil over the pork and cover the dish tightly with heavy-duty aluminum foil. Roast for 4 hours. The pork is now confit.

To make rillettes, drain off the oil and reserve. Transfer the meat to the bowl of a standing mixer with a paddle attachment. Turn on low and let the attachment pound the meat into a soft paste. Add the crème fraîche; fold in the apricots and pistachios. Transfer to an earthenware crock or any airtight container. Pour a thin layer of the cooking fat (discard the rest) over the top, and keep, refrigerated, for up to 1 week.

Option

➤ You could spread the confit on baguette rounds, but I use the confit in pressed sandwiches, such as a Cuban sandwich with Gruyère, pickled jalapeño, and thin slices of ham. It is quite delicious.

Korean Beef and Rice Pot

This is a simple one-pot dish known as *Bi-Bim-Bop*, and a great way to use up leftover rice and vegetables or meat. I fry the eggs, then set them on top of each plate of rice just before serving.

Makes 4 main course servings

2 medium zucchini, julienned

3 tablepoons canola oil

Kosher salt to taste

2 medium carrots, julienned

4 cups spinach

2 cups mung bean sprouts

**8 ounces thinly sliced beef,
    marinated in hoisin sauce**

2 cups cooked basmati rice

4 whole eggs

2 tablespoons unsalted butter

Over medium heat, sauté the zucchini in 1 tablespoon of the canola oil mixed with a little salt. Cover the carrots with boiling water and blanch over medium heat just until tender. Sauté the spinach separately in the remaining canola oil, and cook the bean sprouts in boiling water over medium heat for 20 seconds. Set the vegetables aside separately. Grill the beef briefly, just until cooked through.

Preheat the oven to 300 degrees. Spread ½ cup of rice across the bottom of an ovenproof skillet, and divide the cooked vegetables and beef evenly over the rice. Place the pot over high heat for several minutes, until the rice forms a bottom crust. Move the skillet to the oven for 5 minutes. Divide into four portions, and top each with an egg fried in the hot butter.

Options

➤ If I am feeling lazy, I simply sauté the vegetables and meat together in a giant stir-fry. And if I am even lazier, I make a little nest in the vegetables, crack the egg into the nest, and bake the whole thing in the oven.

➤ Use any vegetable or meat you like, or make it vegetarian by substituting chunks of diced firm tofu.

Grilled Pomegranate Molasses— Glazed Beef Tenderloin

I adore pomegranate molasses; it is made by reducing pomegranate juice. The result is a thick, fruity, sweet-tart molasses which is seriously delicious and versatile—so versatile that I actually use it in a Champagne cocktail: a little pomegranate molasses mixed with a jot of simple syrup topped with your favorite Champagne.

Makes 4 to 6 appetizer servings, or 2 main courses

¼ **cup pomegranate molasses**

2 tablespoons honey

1 teaspoon ground toasted cumin seeds

1 clove garlic, minced

Salt and freshly ground black pepper to taste

2 beef filet mignons, 1½ to 2 inches thick, trimmed well, about ¾ pound

2 to 3 tablespoons canola oil

In a bowl, combine the pomegranate molasses, honey, cumin, garlic, salt, and pepper.

Preheat the oven to 425 degrees.

Place a grill pan over high heat for 5 minutes. Season the filet mignons with a little salt and pepper, and brush with a little oil, about 1 tablespoon in all. Sear the steaks in the grill pan for 2 minutes, then turn them and glaze with a little of the molasses mixture. After 2 minutes turn the filets and glaze them again. Continue in this manner until all sides of the steaks have been seared and glazed. Remove the beef to a baking sheet, brush liberally with the glaze, and place it in the oven. Roast for 2 to 4 minutes for medium-rare. Allow the meat to rest before slicing.

Options

➤ Layer thinly sliced beef, Tina's Pickled Eggplant (page 79), and crumbled feta cheese on flat bread or store-bought pizza crust, such as Boboli. Serve either warm or at room temperature.

➤ Glaze lamb chops with the pomegranate molasses glaze, grill the chops, and serve them with white bean puree and grilled vegetables.

➤ This glaze is also great on venison and chicken.

➤ Brush grilled eggplant with pomegranate molasses glaze, then drizzle with a little yogurt for a quick side dish.

Braised Oxtails with Miso and Black Bean

This rustic dish is great in the wintertime. It is especially rich, meaty, and filling, and it's even better the next day, when the flavors have been allowed to meld and you can easily skim any excess congealed fat off the top. Serve this stew with potato puree flavored with freshly grated horseradish. Ask your butcher to cut the oxtails into 2-inch pieces. The first part of the recipe requires overnight marination, so plan accordingly.

Makes 6 servings

4 tablespoons fermented black beans, soaked in warm water for 15 minutes, drained

¼ cup chopped ginger

5 cloves garlic, peeled

Grated zest of 1 orange

6 to 7 pounds oxtails, cut into 2-inch pieces

½ cup canola oil

3 carrots, cut into large chunks

1 cup pearl onions or 2 onions, cut into large dice

4 stalks celery, cut into large pieces

1 jalapeño pepper, stemmed

1 cup red wine

Water or stock as needed

1 cup dark miso

The day before making the stew, puree the black beans, ginger, garlic, and orange zest in a food processor. Rub the puree over the oxtails, cover, and refrigerate overnight.

In a heavy-bottomed pan large enough to hold all the ingredients, heat the canola oil over high heat. Brown the oxtails in batches and set them aside.

In the same pan, caramelize the carrots, pearl onions, celery, and jalapeño. Return the meat to the pan, add the wine, enough stock or water to come halfway up the meat and miso. Cover, bring to a boil over high heat. Reduce the heat to low and simmer for 4 hours. (Or you can place the covered pot in a preheated 350-degree oven for 4 to 5 hours.) Check from time to time to make sure there is enough liquid in the pot.

Options

➤ Pick the meat off the bone, roll in crêpes, line them up in a baking pan, and bake with a little cheese on top for an easy cannelloni dish.

➤ Serve with steamed rice or noodles instead of potato puree.

➤ If you are on a low-carb diet, try serving the oxtails on a white bean puree (recipe is in my *Cooking from A to Z*) or Smoky Eggplant and Yogurt Puree (page 34).

Fish and Shellfish

Many people are afraid to cook fish. What if it stinks up your home? Most of the fish dishes in this chapter are baked in parchment or steamed, so you don't have to worry about splatters or odors. Besides being utterly delicious, more and more studies are confirming the remarkable salubrious effects of eating plenty of fish.

Kedgeree

Here's an Asian spin on a Scottish recipe that usually includes smoked haddock, hard-boiled eggs, rice, and yes, curry powder. A Scottish regiment stationed in India tried blending the flavors of smoked fish and curry and it worked beautifully.

I serve this as a side dish in the restaurant. It was originally intended as a supper or brunch dish.

Makes 4 smallish servings

2 tablespoons canola oil, possibly more

1 small onion, finely diced

2 tablespoons finely diced ginger

2 cloves garlic, minced

1 tablespoon turmeric powder

1 tablespoon Madras curry powder

Salt and freshly ground black pepper to taste

2 cups basmati rice

2 cups water

2 cups fish stock (optional—you can use all water)

1 cup frozen peas, thawed and warmed

4 hard-boiled eggs, peeled and chopped, at room temperature

1 cup roughly chopped cilantro leaves

12 ounces poached salmon, carefully boned and broken into chunks, warm or at room temperature

Juice of 1 lemon

To a heavy-bottomed saucepot with a tight-fitting lid, add the oil. Place over medium heat and sweat the onion, ginger, and garlic until the onion is translucent. Add the turmeric, curry powder, salt, and pepper. Continue cooking for 5 minutes, stirring judiciously.

Stir in the rice, adding more oil if necessary to coat every grain. Make sure the rice is well coated with the oil and seasonings. Add the liquid(s) and bring to a boil over high heat. Promptly reduce the heat to low and place the lid firmly on the pot. Simmer gently for 15 minutes.

Once the rice is cooked, fluff it gently (I like using a pair of chopsticks). Fold in the peas, chopped egg, cilantro, and salmon chunks. Add the lemon juice.

Grilled Sea Scallops with Pickled Shallots and Green Mango

If you don't want to use shallots in this dish, use a sweet onion like Vidalia or Maui instead. If you can only get a regular Spanish onion, slice it, then soak it in iced water for half an hour before adding the salt.

Makes 3 to 4 servings

½ cup thinly sliced shallots

1 teaspoon kosher salt

1 tablespoon granulated sugar

2 tablespoons rice wine vinegar

10 sea scallops

1 green mango, julienned

½ cup halved cherry tomatoes

½ cup fresh mint leaves

1 tablespoon brown sugar

1 tablespoon Thai fish sauce

Juice of 1 lime

2 tablespoons chopped toasted
   peanuts

Place the shallots in a bowl, add the salt, and allow to stand for 30 minutes. Rinse the shallots under cold water and press out the excess liquid. Transfer to a bowl, add the sugar and vinegar, mix, and allow to marinate for 10 minutes before use.

Grill the scallops until medium-rare, about 1 to 2 minutes per side. Add the shallots, mango, cherry tomatoes, and mint. Toss to combine. In a separate bowl, whisk together the brown sugar, fish sauce, and lime juice. Pour the dressing over the scallop mixture, toss to mix, and sprinkle with the peanuts.

Options

➤ Use shrimp instead of scallops.

➤ Use jicama instead of green mango.

➤ I sometimes add a little grated garlic to the brown sugar, fish sauce, and lime juice mixture, to give it a little more depth and a bite.

➤ Blanched cellophane noodles can be added to give it more bulk.

Crackling Rice Paper—Wrapped Cod

Actually, you can use whatever fish you prefer. I like using cod because it's so accessible and inexpensive. But you may find halibut a little firmer and easier to handle. Or you could use monkfish, turbot, red snapper, or even salmon.

Makes 4 servings

4 pieces cod, 4 to 5 ounces each

2 tablespoons ginger juice

1 tablespoon soy sauce

1 tablespoon mirin (sweetened rice wine)

4 cups water

½ cup golden beer

1 tablespoon sugar

Salt to taste

4 sheets rice paper, in 8-inch rounds

1½ tablespoons chopped cilantro leaves

2 tablespoons canola oil

In a bowl, combine the cod with the ginger juice, soy, and mirin. Marinate the cod while you prepare the rice paper.

In a shallow pan over high heat, bring the water to a boil with the beer, sugar, and salt. Turn off the heat.

Spread out a clean kitchen towel on a flat surface. Place a sheet of rice paper in the warm beer solution and let it soften for 1 minute. Remove the rice paper and place it on the kitchen towel. Put two or three cilantro leaves in the center of the rice paper, place a piece of fish over the herb, then fold the rice paper over the fish to form a package. Repeat with all the rice paper and fish. (These packages can be made up to a day in advance, but they must be well wrapped in plastic wrap and refrigerated.)

Ten minutes before serving, sauté the packages in the canola oil over medium heat until golden brown, about 3 to 5 minutes on each side.

Options

➤ Serve these golden rice paper packages over a Green Mango Salad (page 4).

➤ For lunch, serve these packages with thick pieces of taro chips, as a variation on fish and chips.

➤ Make a dipping sauce of the Indonesian condiment *sambal,* fresh lime juice, and a little simple syrup, and serve it on the side.

Halibut Baked in Parchment with Porcini and Sherry Butter

Wrapping fish in parchment is one of my favorite ways to cook it. It's the ideal cooking method if you don't have a dishwasher because the container in which you are cooking is entirely disposable. Foil works really well too, but parchment is more dramatic because the paper browns and turns brittle and you can present the packages to your guests to open up and release the fragrant steam.

Makes 4 servings

1 leek, cleaned well and cut crosswise into ⅛-inch pieces

4 to 5 tablespoons canola oil

2 tablespoons thyme

4 large shiitake mushrooms, stemmed and julienned

1 portobello mushroom, stemmed, "gills" scraped away, and julienned

¼ cup chanterelle, morel, or black trumpet mushrooms (optional)

1 shallot, thinly sliced

Salt and freshly ground black pepper to taste

1 teaspoon crushed red pepper flakes

4 sheets parchment paper, 1 foot square

4 pieces halibut, 4 to 5 ounces each

4 ounces Porcini and Sherry Butter, softened (page 76)

¼ cup dry white wine

Preheat the oven to 350 degrees.

In a skillet over medium heat, sweat the leek in 2 tablespoons of the canola oil with the thyme. Reserve.

Toss all the mushrooms and the shallot with the remaining 2 to 3 tablespoons of the canola oil, season with salt and the red pepper flakes. Spread on a cookie sheet and bake for 10 to 15 minutes, until the mushrooms start to brown. Reserve. Raise the oven to 400 degrees.

Lay a piece of parchment on a flat surface. Spread a quarter of the leek mixture on half of the parchment, and top with a piece of halibut. Season the fish lightly with salt and pepper, spread a quarter of the

Porcini and Sherry Butter on each piece of fish, and top with a quarter of the roasted mushrooms. Moisten with the wine, fold the parchment over, and seal the edges by folding. Repeat for all the fish. Bake the packages on a baking sheet for 15 minutes. Serve immediately.

Options

➤ If you don't want to bake the fish in parchment, lay it in an ovenproof dish or gratin, cover the dish with foil, and bake for 15 minutes.

➤ This cooking method works for any fish, and the flavoring that you use in the parchment can vary. Some of my favorite variations include heirloom tomatoes, olives, and capers with Lemon Butter (page 75), and summer squash and eggplant with sundried tomato butter (1 stick unsalted butter, softened, and stirred with 10 chopped, drained oil-packed sundried tomatoes).

➤ Try cooking chicken in parchment, just lengthen the cooking time to 30 to 40 minutes.

Poached Prawn and Tomato Confit Stack

All my restaurants have been located near prime shopping areas or in business districts, so this dish was developed for "the ladies who lunch." But it became so popular that we always moved it to the dinner menu too. A miniature version using pear tomatoes is great to serve at cocktail parties.

Makes 10 stacks, 10 appetizer servings, 5 main course servings

**15 plum tomatoes, halved lengthwise
     and seeded**

2 cloves garlic, thinly sliced

1 teaspoon crushed red pepper flakes

¼ cup canola oil

**Salt and freshly ground black pepper
     to taste**

20 poached prawns

1 cup Salsa Verde (page 84)

Preheat the oven to 200 degrees.

Toss the tomatoes with the garlic, pepper flakes, canola oil, and season with salt and pepper. Roast on a rack over a parchment-lined sheet for 1 hour. The tomatoes should caramelize slightly but also dry out a bit at the same time. Let cool. The tomato skin should peel off easily at this point. (It isn't absolutely necessary to peel the tomato, but it does taste better when the slightly leathery skin is removed.)

Halve the prawns lengthwise, toss them with the Salsa Verde, and season well. Stack two pieces of prawns on a tomato half. Repeat until there are two layers of shrimp and three layers of tomatoes. Repeat. Serve at room temperature on a small green salad.

Options

➤ Layer the roasted tomatoes with crab salad, chicken salad, or even egg salad.

➤ Serve the stacks on a small salad of avocado and cucumber with a lemony mayonnaise.

➤ If you want to get really fancy, layer the roasted tomatoes with slices of grilled lobster.

Clam Fritters

I am a big fan of fried clams and of clam chowder. This recipe is a hybrid of both of these favorites. You can buy freshly shucked clams from a reputable fishmonger.

Makes about 30 small fritters

1 cup shucked clams

½ cup each diced, cooked Yukon gold potatoes and russet potatoes

1 onion, diced

1 stalk celery, diced

½ roasted poblano chile, diced

½ cup all-purpose flour

½ cup potato flakes (instant potatoes)

2 tablespoons baking powder

½ cup buttermilk

Canola oil for frying

Combine all the ingredients except the oil in a large bowl and mix well. Drop 1 tablespoonful at a time into 1 to 2 inches of 375-degree oil, and fry over medium-high heat for 3 minutes on each side until golden brown. Serve immediately.

Option

➤ Serve with avocado butter: equal parts soft butter, ripe avocado flesh, and freshly squeezed lime juice to taste.

Cured Salmon Club Sandwich
on Brioche with Chipotle Puree

This really fancy sandwich makes for a great Sunday brunch with your mum. Just buy the best-quality Nova smoked salmon you can find, or if you feel up to it you can cure your own. Use brioche or challah bread; both are delicate and eggy. Chipotle peppers canned in adobo sauce are pretty widely available now. You may have noticed how much I like them!

Makes 2 servings

½ cup cream cheese, softened

1 scallion, green part only, roughly chopped

6 slices lightly toasted brioche or challah bread

6 slices cured salmon

1 red onion, thinly sliced

1 beefsteak tomato, cut into ½-inch slices

1 small cucumber, thinly sliced

1 ripe Haas avocado, peeled, pitted, and mashed

2 tablespoons pureed, canned chipotle peppers in adobo

Puree the cream cheese and scallions together. Spread on two slices of the toasted brioche, then top with two slices of the cured salmon. Top each sandwich with another slice of brioche. On top of this, stack the onion, tomato, cucumber, and mashed avocado. Top each sandwich with the last slices of brioche, spread with the chipotle puree. Secure with skewers.

Options

➢ Pile the ingredients on a toasted bagel and eat it while reading the Sunday paper.

➢ Omit the cream cheese and avocado and serve over a green salad.

Grilled Squid with Giant White Beans in a Green Olive Vinaigrette

Gigante beans are large dried white beans from Greece. Their chestnuty texture complements grilled squid quite well, and a nice green olive vinaigrette brings the whole dish together, giving it a piquant flavor. If you don't want to pit and chop your own green olives, use jarred green olive tapanade. I like making my own because I can control the texture of the vinaigrette.

Makes 4 servings

1 pound squid

Salt and freshly ground black pepper to taste

Canola oil for frying (optional)

2 cups cooked *gigante* beans

¼ cup roughly chopped fresh oregano leaves

1 red onion, thinly sliced

1 cup blanched cut-up green beans (trimmed and cut into 1-inch lengths)

1 serrano chile, stemmed and sliced crosswise into thin rounds

1 clove garlic, peeled

1 cup pitted green olives (if possible, use a mixture of picholine and Cerignola)

½ cup Champagne vinegar

Heat a grill to high, or heat a grill pan over high heat. Clean the squid, keeping the bodies whole. Season with salt and pepper and grill for 2 minutes on each side, or fry in canola oil for 2 minutes per side. Cut the squid into bite-sized pieces and transfer them to a bowl with the beans, oregano, onion, green beans, and chile.

In a miniprocessor, mince the garlic clove, then add the olives and vinegar. Puree until you get the texture you want. Pour over the squid, toss the mixture, and allow to marinate for a few minutes before serving.

Squid "Pasta" with Black Bean Paste

This stir-fry is both flavorful and simple to make. As with most stir-fried dishes, the only real labor comes in the preparation of the ingredients. I like to serve this as a garnish for a piece of sautéed or grilled fish like cod or halibut, but it is just as good served on steamed white rice.

Makes 4 servings

¼ cup fermented black beans, soaked in warm water for 10 minutes

4 cloves garlic, finely chopped

2 tablespoons finely chopped ginger

1 fresh jalapeño pepper, finely chopped

1 tablespoon canola oil

1 pound cleaned squid bodies, sliced into really thin spaghetti-sized strips

½ cup thinly sliced celery stalks

1 cup cherry tomatoes, halved

Juice of ½ lemon

Salt and freshly ground black pepper to taste

2 tablespoons chopped cilantro or parsley

Drain the black beans and roughly chop them, then combine them with the garlic, ginger, and jalapeño. In a very hot sauté pan or wok over high heat, heat the canola oil. Add the black bean mixture and cook, stirring until fragrant. Add the squid, celery, and cherry tomatoes, and stir-fry for 2 minutes. Season with the lemon juice, salt, and pepper (remember fermented black beans are salty, so be careful with the salt), add the chopped herb, and serve immediately.

Option

➤ I also like serving this squid pasta with Mediterranean flavors: Instead of the black bean mixture, try tossing the squid with olives, capers, and sun-dried tomatoes.

Angel-Hair Pasta with Peekytoe Crab, Garlic, and Chili

This is a tasty variation on one of my favorite pasta dishes. Traditionally, this pasta is made with sardines, but I realize that fresh sardines are not only a nuisance to clean, but there is such a stigma against them—however unwarranted—that we use crabmeat instead. Substitute rice noodles for the angel-hair to give the dish an Asian flair.

Makes 4 servings

1 pound angel-hair pasta

¼ cup olive oil

4 cloves garlic, peeled and finely chopped

2 anchovy fillets, soaked in milk for 10 minutes, then finely chopped

2 teaspoons crushed red pepper flakes

1 pound asparagus, trimmed, peeled if thick, and cut crosswise into ¼-inch rounds, about 2 cups

1 pound peekytoe crabmeat, picked over carefully for bits of shell or cartilage

1 cup halved cherry tomatoes

½ cup white wine (optional), or ¼ to ½ cup pasta water

1 cup basil leaves, roughly torn

Cook the pasta according to package directions. While the pasta is cooking, heat a large, deep sauté pan with ¼ cup olive oil over high heat. Add the garlic and quickly reduce the heat to medium, stirring constantly to make sure the garlic does not burn. Add the anchovies, red pepper flakes, and asparagus, and cook for 1 minute. Stir in the crabmeat and cherry tomatoes. At this point, you may give the mixture a splash of white wine (or ¼ to ½ cup of the pasta water), to loosen the mixture. Add the pasta and basil and toss well.

Steamed Mussels with Green Curry Broth

This dish is really simple to make, it's packed full of flavors, and has quite a dramatic presentation. If you don't like mussels, use clams or a combination of both shellfish.

Makes 2 servings

24 mussels

2 tablespoons canola oil

¼ cup diced onion

2 cloves garlic, chopped

1 tablespoon Thai green curry paste

1 cup dry white wine

Cilantro sprigs for garnish

**2 thick slices grilled sourdough
   bread**

Scrub the mussels well. In a large sauté pan with a tight-fitting lid, add the canola oil over medium heat. Caramelize the onion for 5 minutes, then add the garlic and curry paste. Sauté for 2 minutes until fragrant. Add the mussels and white wine. Cover the pan tightly and allow the mussels to cook for about 5 minutes. Dispose of any unopened mussels. Garnish with cilantro and serve immediately with the grilled bread.

Option

➤ Try baking the mussels wrapped in parchment in a preheated 400-degree oven for 10 minutes. Cut the bag open at the table for a really dramatic and very fragrant presentation.

Baked Mussels and Spinach with Orange-Saffron Mayonnaise

I like serving this dish in small gratin dishes either as a light lunch with crusty grilled bread and a crisp green salad or as a side dish with pieces of sautéed fillets of rouget or skate. Prepare it ahead of time and it is a snap to serve for dinner parties. To make Orange-Saffron Mayonnaise, refer to the recipe for Chipotle Mayonnaise (page 70), and simply replace the chipotle with the grated rind of 1 orange and a pinch of saffron soaked in 2 tablespoons of warm water.

Makes 4 servings

5 pounds mussels

1 cup roughly chopped carrots

1 cup roughly chopped onion

1 cup roughly chopped celery
   stalks

½ cup white wine

1 cup dried bread crumbs

Grated zests of 1 orange and
   1 lemon

1 cup finely chopped parsley

2 cloves garlic, peeled and finely
   chopped

2 cups cooked spinach (frozen
   spinach is fine—you'll need
   2 pounds of fresh loose spinach to
   make 2 cups of cooked)

1 cup Orange-Saffron Mayonnaise
   (see Headnote above)

Preheat the oven to 400 degrees.

Put the mussels, carrots, onion, and celery in a large pot with a tight-fitting lid. Add the white wine and place over high heat for 10 minutes, or until the mussels open. Discard the vegetables and any unopened mussels, but reserve the liquid.

Remove the mussels from their shells and reserve. Mix together the bread crumbs, zests, parsley, and garlic. Lightly butter an ovenproof dish. Spread the spinach on the bottom and nestle the mussels evenly over the top. Spread with a thin layer of the orange-saffron mayonnaise and top with bread-crumb mixture. Bake for 10 minutes or until warmed through.

Turmeric-Scented Crab and Fish Cake

Crab and fish cakes are quintessentially American. This recipe calls for a combination of both fish and shellfish, lightly scented with the turmeric, galangal, and a little ginger. The bite of the three different varieties of ginger beautifully complements the sweetness of the fish and crab.

Makes 5 to 6 servings

1 8-ounce piece fresh, skinned cod
(see Options below)

1 medium onion, diced

1 stalk celery, diced

1 fresh jalapeño pepper, diced

1 tablespoon grated turmeric (see
Options below)

2 tablespoons grated galangal

2 tablespoons grated fresh ginger

1 cup crabmeat, picked over to
remove any pieces of shell or
cartilage

¼ cup mayonnaise

Grated zest of 2 lemons

½ cup bread crumbs

Salt and freshly ground black pepper
to taste

Flour for dusting

2 eggs, beaten

1 cup *panko* (firm Japanese bread
crumbs)

Canola oil for frying

Poach the cod in simmering salt water for 10 minutes. Cool, flake, and set aside. In a roomy skillet over medium heat, sweat the onion, celery, and jalapeño with the turmeric, galangal, and ginger. Let the mixture cool, then stir in the crabmeat and flaked cod. Fold in the mayonnaise, lemon zests, bread crumbs, salt, and pepper. Form the mixture into cakes 2 inches in diameter and about ½ inch thick. Set up three bowls, one with the flour, the second with the beaten eggs, and the third with the *panko*. Dust each crab cake with the flour, dip into the beaten eggs, then in the *panko*. Sauté the cakes in the canola oil over medium heat until golden brown. Serve immediately.

Options

➢ Try using reconstituted salt cod
instead of fresh cod. Soak the
salt cod for 3 days, refrigerated,
changing the water 3 times a
day. The fish cake will have a little more depth, but be careful
when adding salt to the mixture.

➢ If you are unable to find the
root, use ¼ teaspoon turmeric
powder.

➢ Leave out the ginger, turmeric,
and galangal, and use another
flavoring, such as a tablespoon
of Harissa (page 72), or just
leave the mixture plain.

Vegetables and
Side Dishes

I've tried to enliven the often ho-hum second fiddlers to make these accompaniments worthy of standing front and center. There's no excuse for boring side dishes!

Creamy Potato Puree, with Variations

Even in this age of low-carb diets, creamy mashed potatoes remain a perennial favorite. You could probably come up with a different variation on mashed potatoes for every day of the year. Here are just a few of my favorites. If you just want to make straight mashed potatoes, experiment with different types of potatoes. A mealy, high-starch potato like a russet or Idaho potato will result in a puree that is completely different from a waxy potato like Yukon gold or Red Bliss.

Makes 4 servings

Basic Creamy Potato Puree

**4 large russet potatoes, peeled and
   cut in half**
Salt
½ cup (1 stick) butter
2 cups milk
Freshly ground black pepper to taste

Cover the potatoes with water, add enough salt to make the water taste mildly salty, and boil until tender, about 20 minutes, while you melt the butter in the milk over medium heat. Drain the potatoes and return them to the pot. Dry the potatoes in the pot over medium heat for a minute or two, then pass them through a food mill or a potato ricer. If you do not have either apparatus, mash them really well. Do not put the potatoes into a food processor. Pour the buttered milk into the mashed potatoes, stirring, just until you reach the texture you want. Season with the salt and pepper.

Options

➤ Try steaming two peeled potatoes with a medium head of
cauliflower cut into medium florets or peeled and chopped celery root until tender, about half
an hour. Steaming the vegetables prevents them from becom-
ing water-logged, and they do
tend to lose their flavor in the
liquid. Mash the potatoes and
puree the cauliflower. Fold together with the butter and milk.
Serve with parchment-wrapped
salmon (page 136).

➤ I like to add lots of peeled,
crushed garlic to my potatoes
while they are boiling.

➤ Flavor plain potatoes with some
horseradish, and serve them
with braised short ribs.

Spiced Chili Potatoes

I am quite a fan of these potatoes. They're a cross between a potato curry and roasted potatoes, and they make the perfect side for roasted meats. I usually make a really large batch, because any leftovers are wonderful in potato salad the next day, or they may be baked with a little cheese to accompany a green salad for an easy lunch.

Makes 6 servings

1 tablespoon gold mustard seeds

1 tablespoon black mustard seeds

4 Thai bird chilies, kept whole

½ teaspoon curry powder

¼ cup canola oil or other unflavored oil

1 onion, cut into ¼-inch-thick slices

2 large russet potatoes, peeled and cut into ½-inch slices

4 large Yukon gold potatoes, peeled and cut into ½-inch slices

Salt and freshly ground black pepper to taste

½ cup chicken stock (or just plain water)

2 tablespoons unsalted butter, cut into ¼-inch pieces

1 tablespoon yogurt or sour cream

Chopped cilantro for garnish

Preheat the oven to 375 degrees.

In a dry cast-iron pan over high heat, toast the mustard seeds, chilies, and curry powder, stirring until the mustard seeds begin to pop, 2 to 3 minutes. Carefully add the oil and onion. Cook, stirring, until the onion caramelizes and turns dark brown.

Toss the potatoes with the salt and pepper and add them to the pan with the chicken stock. Dot the top of the potatoes with the butter and bake for 20 to 25 minutes. I usually serve this right in the pan with an additional dollop of yogurt. Garnish with the chopped cilantro.

Note: Fish out the Thai bird chilies halfway through the cooking process if you don't want the potatoes to be too spicy. If you leave them in the pan throughout the roasting, be sure to warn your guests not to eat them unless they have a death wish. Thai bird chilies are truly incendiary.

Malaysian Fried Rice

There are as many variations of fried rice as there are cooks. It is simply a way to use up excess steamed rice, and surprisingly enough, fried rice is much better made with cold rice that has been sitting around for a day in the refrigerator. This is a very basic *nasi goreng*, Malay for fried rice.

Makes 4 to 6 servings

3 to 4 tablespoons canola oil

2 cups cold cooked rice

1 egg, beaten

1 teaspoon freshly ground Sichuan pepper

Salt to taste

3 to 4 scallions, green parts only, sliced crosswise into ⅛-inch rings, for garnish

Place the canola oil in a heavy-bottomed sauté pan or wok over medium-high heat. When the oil is very hot, carefully add the rice, and stir until the rice is coated with the oil and starts to pop. Quickly add the beaten egg to the rice, stirring rapidly to coat the rice with the egg until the mixture is fairly dry. Season with the pepper and salt, and serve garnished with the scallions.

Options

➢ To serve *nasi goreng* as a main course, simply add whatever you may have on hand—julienned vegetables, and/or diced roasted chicken, pork, or lamb.

➢ Serve *nasi goreng* with poached shrimp or cubed poached salmon.

➢ True Indonesian *nasi goreng* calls for the use of *kecap manis*, which is basically a sweetened, reduced soy sauce. I find that the *kecap manis* makes the rice a little too sweet, but if you like your rice slightly sweet, by all means stir in a tablespoon.

Vegetables and Side Dishes

Rice Pilaf

One of my favorite—and most versatile—side dishes is this very fragrant and flavorful Rice Pilaf.

Make 4 to 6 servings

2 tablespoons canola oil, or

   1 tablespoon oil and 1 tablespoon

   butter

1 medium onion, diced

1 cup basmati or long-grain white

   rice, rinsed in several changes of

   cold water until water is clear

2 cups chicken stock

1 cinnamon stick

1 star anise

2 cardamom pods, cracked

6 to 8 saffron threads

2 imported bay leaves

Salt to taste

Place the oil into a heavy-bottomed saucepan over medium-high heat. Sauté the onion until it's translucent. Add the rice and sauté until each grain of rice is well coated with the oil, adding more oil if necessary. Add the remaining ingredients, and bring to a boil. Reduce the heat to the lowest setting possible, and put a tight-fitting lid on the saucepan. (If you don't have a tight-fitting lid, cover the saucepan tightly with heavy-duty foil.) Cook for ½ hour, or until all the liquid has evaporated and the rice is cooked. Uncover and fluff the rice before serving. Remove the cinnamon stick, star anise, cardamom pods, and bay leaves. I like fluffing my rice with a pair of chopsticks—it doesn't break up the grains as much as using a spoon or fork.

Options

➢ I sometimes add diced dried fruit such as apricots or currants to my pilaf, as well as toasted pistachios, just before serving.

➢ Stir poached small shrimp or pieces of diced ham into the cooked rice.

➢ I like serving pilaf with stews or fairly spicy grilled meats or fish.

Coconut Rice Croquettes

There is a rice dish common in Malaysia, Indonesia, and Singapore called *nasi lemak*, which literally means creamy rice. These croquettes are a cross between that rice dish and *arancini*, which is an Italian risotto cake.

Makes 4 servings

1 cup basmati rice

1 cup unsweetened coconut milk

½ cup water

2 teaspoons salt

1 stick cinnamon

Canola oil for frying

Preheat the oven to 350 degrees.

In a colander rinse the rice well in cold running water until the water runs clear after passing through the rice. Mix the coconut milk and water together with salt. In an ovenproof heavy-bottomed pot with a tight-fitting lid, blend the rice, coconut milk, and cinnamon stick. Over high heat bring the mixture to a rolling boil. Do not stir the rice once it is cooking, as that tends to break up the grains, making the rice gummy. Cover the pot tightly, remove it from the stove, and bake for 15 minutes in the oven.

Form the cooled rice into croquettes, I like making mine about ½ inch thick and about 2 inches in diameter. If you make them too large, the center never warms up completely without the outside getting too brown. Pan-fry the croquettes in about 1 inch of canola oil at about 375 degrees.

Options

➤ Serve these croquettes as a side dish with a curry.

➤ Or you can make the croquettes a little smaller and serve them with your favorite chutney as an hors d'oeuvre for 6 to 8 people.

Smoky Tomato Polenta

When I tell people that I like polenta, they often wrinkle their noses at me. Some people think polenta is passé, "very eighties." Those people don't know what they're missing! I make my polenta with stone-ground white cornmeal, which tastes especially nutty. I am almost embarrassed to give you this recipe because it is so simple. I use good-quality canned tomatoes for this, such as Muir Glen or San Marzano. Fresh tomatoes are almost too watery and they rarely seem to develop the intense flavors of the canned.

Makes 4 to 6 servings

1 (14-ounce) can whole Italian plum tomatoes, or whole Muir Glen organic tomatoes

4 cloves garlic, peeled and roughly chopped

2 shallots, thinly sliced

Salt and freshly ground black pepper to taste

1 cup white cornmeal

1 cup chicken stock or water

1 cup half-and-half (or milk, if you prefer)

½ cup crème fraîche

Preheat the oven to 350 degrees.

Drain the liquid from the tomatoes, toss with the garlic and shallots, and season well with the salt and pepper. Spread the tomatoes on a cookie sheet. Roast in the oven for 1 hour, stirring often, allowing the flavors to intensify. Let the tomatoes cool, then roughly chop them up (I just squeeze them with my hands, breaking up the large pieces and throwing away the hard core). Set aside.

Pour the cornmeal, stock, and milk into a heavy-bottomed pot. Place over high heat, and stir the mixture constantly. Once the mixture comes to a boil, reduce the heat to low and cook for a half hour, stirring from time to time so that the polenta doesn't burn at the bottom of the pan. Fold in the tomatoes and crème fraîche. Serve immediately.

Options

➢ Some cooks heat the liquid, then add the cornmeal in a thin stream so it doesn't become lumpy, but I find that stirring the mixture while the liquid comes to a boil works better. If your polenta is lumpy, simply strain it to remove the lumps.

➢ Allow any leftover polenta to set; cut it into blocks and sauté in butter. Serve for brunch with soft scrambled eggs with nuggets of goat cheese folded in.

Linguini with Roasted Cauliflower, Bacon, and Pine Nuts

My brother-in-law John hated cauliflower until I made him taste it roasted one day. Roasting mellows out the cruciferous odor and caramelizes the natural sugar in the vegetable, making it really yummy. Try roasting other cruciferous vegetables like Brussels sprouts and broccoli as well.

Makes 4 servings

1 pound linguini (see Options below)

1 head cauliflower, cut into bite-size florets

2 tablespoons canola oil (or more, if the cauliflower is large)

Salt and freshly ground black pepper to taste

½ cup diced slab bacon (see Options below)

1 onion, diced

1 clove garlic, finely chopped

2 tablespoons fresh thyme leaves

½ cup toasted pine nuts (see Options below)

Extra-virgin olive oil for drizzling (optional)

Preheat the oven to 350 degrees.

Cook the pasta according to package instructions. Toss the cauliflower with the canola oil, season with the salt and pepper, and roast for 10 to 15 minutes. Stir from time to time, making sure that the cauliflower does not burn.

While the cauliflower is cooking, sauté the bacon with the onion, garlic, and thyme until the onion is golden brown. Add the roasted cauliflower to the bacon mixture and toss it with the pasta. Sprinkle with the toasted pine nuts. Drizzle with some extra-virgin olive oil, if desired.

Options

➤ Use a mixture of roasted cauliflower, Brussels sprouts, and
broccoli.

➤ Leave out the bacon if you want
to make the pasta vegetarian.

➤ Substitute croutons for the pine
nuts.

➤ Leave out the pasta and serve
the roasted cauliflower and bacon mixture as a side with a
roasted chicken.

➤ Roughly chop up the cauli-
flower/bacon mixture and use it
as a filling for ravioli.

Wild Mushroom Risotto

Risotto is not particularly Asian, even though rice in many forms is a staple of Asian diets. This dish is inspired by a side dish I once had in Japan consisting of steamed sticky rice and matsutake mushrooms. Matsutake mushrooms are also known as pine mushrooms, and can be found throughout the Pacific Northwest and northeastern America. They are piney, woody, and really meaty.

Makes 8 servings

4 tablespoons canola oil

1 shallot, finely diced

2 cups diced cremini mushrooms

1¾ cups arborio rice

4 cups sake

9 cups mushroom stock

1 cup good sherry (I like
   Amontillado)

Pour 2 tablespoons of the canola oil into a large heavy-bottomed skillet over medium-high heat. Add the shallot and mushrooms and sauté until the mushrooms are dark brown and caramelized. Add the rice and the remaining 2 tablespoons of canola oil. Toast the rice, stirring to make sure each grain is well coated with the oil. Add the sake. Stir and reduce the heat to medium. Keep stirring until all the sake is absorbed. Add the stock 1 cup at a time, stirring constantly. As each cup of liquid is absorbed add more liquid until the rice is al dente. After all the liquid is absorbed, add the sherry. Stir once and serve immediately.

Option

➢ The alcohol in the sherry will not have a chance to cook off, so if you don't want to use alcohol, leave the sherry out. Try adding 2 tablespoons of almond or walnut oil instead.

Roasted Cauliflower, Green Chili, and Crab Custard

This is a savory custard, an adaptation of *chawan mushi*, which is a really light Japanese custard.

Makes 6 servings

1 cup cauliflower florets

1 shallot, thinly sliced

2 tablespoons canola oil or other flavorless oil

Salt and freshly ground black pepper to taste

8 large eggs

4 ounces chicken or vegetable stock

2 poblano chilies, roasted, blackened skin rubbed off, stemmed, seeded, and sliced ½ cup crabmeat, picked over carefully to find and remove any shell or cartilage fragments

Preheat the oven to 350 degrees.

Toss the cauliflower with the shallot, canola oil, and seasoning. Roast in the oven for 15 minutes until tender and slightly caramelized. Let cool.

Depending on what texture you prefer (I like mine fairly chunky), roughly chop or puree the roasted cauliflower. Beat the eggs lightly with the stock, then add the cauliflower and the remaining ingredients. Combine well. Transfer to six 6-ounce custard cups.

Steam in a steamer for 15 minutes, or place in a covered water bath, and bake in the 350-degree oven for 20 minutes or until the custard sets.

Option

➤ Vary the flavor of the custard. I like corn and shrimp, asparagus, and crab. Just use your favorite combination.

Crispy Spring Onion Rings

Traditionally made with duck fat or lard, these crisp onion rings make the perfect side for a grilled cheese sandwich. They are quite time consuming but well worth the effort. They are actually quite similar to scallion pancakes, just more fun to eat. As with any of the wheat flour–based recipes in this book, this one originated in Northern China.

Makes 4 to 5 servings

2⅔ cups all-purpose flour

Pinch of salt

½ cup shortening or duck fat or butter

¾ cup ice-cold water

1 cup ½-inch-length scallions, green parts only

2 teaspoons canola oil

1 teaspoon sesame oil

Freshly ground black pepper to taste

Canola oil for frying or deep-frying

Sift the flour into a bowl. Add a pinch of salt and work in the shortening until it resembles coarse cornmeal. Add the water and mix the dough. Knead for 10 minutes until it develops a slight sheen. (This can be made in a food processor: Pulse the flour, salt, and shortening together, then add the water through the feed tube while still processing the mixture.) Wrap the dough in plastic and let it rest for 20 minutes.

Mix the green onions, canola oil, and sesame oil together. Season with salt and pepper. Set aside.

Roll the dough into a long rope about 2 inches in diameter. Cut into

8 to 10 pieces. Using a rolling pin,
roll each piece into a small rectangle, about 4 by 6 inches. Place the
green onion mixture in the center,
fold the dough over, pressing lightly
to seal, and join the ends to form a
flattish ring.

Pan-fry or deep-fry the rings in
canola oil until golden brown. Drain
and serve immediately.

Option

➤ Use other vegetables for the filling. Some of my favorites are
ramps (a wild bulb that's a cross
between garlic and leeks), garlic
chives, or leeks.

Bonito-Crusted Tempura for Vegetables

This side dish is great for cocktail parties. Dried bonito tuna flakes (*katsuobushi*) and nori (dried Japanese seaweed) are found in many supermarkets and most Asian food stores. The salty bonito crusts on the vegetables complement cocktails really well.

Basic Tempura Batter (may be halved, doubled, tripled, etc., but see Note below):

- 1 cup all-purpose flour
- 1½ cups club soda
- 1 tablespoon plus 2 teaspoons baking powder
- 1 cup bonito flakes
- ½ cup nori, cut into ¼-inch-thick 1-inch lengths
- Salt and freshly ground black pepper, or cayenne, to taste

Whisk all the ingredients together.

Note: The batter is best when it doesn't sit too long. During the course of a night in the restaurants, we would make the batter two or three times. It's certainly simple enough, and if you premeasure the dry ingredients, all you need to do is add the club soda.

Option

➤ I like using asparagus (pencil asparagus works best), sliced eggplant, sweet potato, mushrooms, and green beans. Experiment with this tempura batter using whatever vegetables you like.

Miso-Grilled Eggplant with Toasted Sesame Seeds

Makes 10 halves, serving 5

1 cup sesame seeds

5 purple japanese eggplants

½ cup light miso

½ cup mirin (sweetened sake; optional)

¼ cup simple syrup (if you are omitting mirin)

½ cup canola oil

Minced scallions for garnishing

In a heavy sauté pan over medium heat, toast the sesame seeds, stirring constantly, until the seeds are golden brown, almost carmel-colored, and very fragrant. Remove to a bowl and set aside.

Cut off the tops of the eggplants, and with a sharp vegetable peeler peel off strips of skin so the eggplants are striped white (where the skin is peeled) and purple (where the skin is not). Cut the eggplants in half lengthwise, and score the cut sides of the eggplants.

Mix the remaining ingredients, except the scallion garnish, together, and toss the eggplant halves in the mixture. Grill on a hot grill for 3 minutes on each side. If the eggplant is large and has not cooked through, simply transfer to a preheated 350-degree oven for another 3 to 4 minutes.

Toss the warm eggplant with the toasted sesame seeds and garnish with scallions.

Vegetables and Side Dishes

Desserts

Grilled Pineapple and Vanilla Ice Cream

I must confess that I don't have much of a sweet tooth. I am one of those people who would rather have an extra serving of mashed potatoes and pass up dessert. But this dessert is perfect because it's quite easy and you can make it as sweet or as savory as you like. Use your favorite fruit—pineapples and pears in the winter, figs and plums in the fall, peaches and nectarines in the summer, and apricots and sautéed cherries in the spring. Use your favorite store-bought ice cream if you do not want to bother making your own.

Makes enough for 4 to 6 desserts

1 pineapple, peeled, cored, and cut into 2-inch rings

½ cup white or dark rum (optional)

2 tablespoons dark brown sugar (optional)

If the pineapple is not terribly ripe, it's best to macerate the fruit in a mixture of the rum and sugar for 10 to 15 minutes before grilling. But if it's ripe enough, you can simply grill the fruit alone. Make sure the grill or grilling pan is very hot before putting on the fruit. Grill the pineapple for 3 to 5 minutes on each side, or until it caramelizes and is nicely browned. Serve immediately.

Options

➤ Grilled pineapple is also delicious diced and tossed with mint or lemon verbena, then served with whipped cream and shortbread biscuits (recipe follows).

➤ Thread the fruit like strawberries or figs onto water-soaked bamboo skewers to make them easier to turn, or put the fruit into a grill basket.

Basic Buttermilk Shortcake Biscuits

I think that there are so many similarities between biscuits and scones that the recipes can practically be used interchangeably. If I decide to serve strawberry shortcake for dessert and am too lazy to make my own biscuits, I just buy scones from my local coffee shop and use them instead—and I am usually too lazy to bake!

Here's a recipe for really basic shortcake biscuits.

Makes about 15 two-inch rounds (but you may prefer other shapes)

6 tablespoons cold unsalted butter, cut into 12 pieces
2 cups all-purpose flour
1 teaspoon baking powder
1 teaspoon baking soda
Pinch of salt
¾ cup buttermilk
¼ cup sugar

Preheat the oven to 350 degrees.

Handle this dough as little as possible. If you are making this by hand, quickly rub the butter into the flour, baking powder, baking soda, and salt, keeping some pieces of butter the size of peas while the rest of the mixture should resemble coarse sand. Add the milk and toss until the mixture holds together. Shape into a rectangle about ½ inch in thickness, wrap tightly with plastic wrap, and refrigerate for at least 15 minutes.

Cut the rectangle into biscuit shapes, brush them with milk, and sprinkle them with sugar. Bake the biscuits on cookie sheets for 10 to 15 minutes or until brown. Serve while still warm with fruit and whipped cream.

Option

➤ To macerate ripe strawberries, wash, dry, and hull them, crush about ¼ of them in a bowl, and slice the rest into the bowl. Stir with a few tablespoons of sugar per pint of strawberries, or more to taste. Let the strawberries macerate for at least a half hour.

Baked Coconut Rice Pudding

Naturally, any Asian-themed restaurant is going to have a *lot* of leftover cooked rice at any given moment. Good cooks hate to waste food, so I came up with an Asian-accented rice pudding that uses up 1½ cups of cooked rice.

Makes 6 servings

1 to 2 tablespoons softened unsalted butter

2 large eggs

⅓ cup sugar

Grated zest of 1 lime

¼ teaspoon ground cloves

¼ teaspoon ground cinnamon

¼ teaspoon salt

1 cup coconut milk

½ cup whole milk

1½ cups cooked Jasmine rice

½ cup golden raisins, plumped in hot water for 20 minutes (see Options below)

1 teaspoon almond extract

Preheat the oven to 350 degrees.

Butter six 6-ounce ramekins. Whisk together the eggs, sugar, lime zest, cloves, cinnamon, and salt until well blended and smooth.

Bring the coconut milk and whole milk to a simmer, and temper the egg mixture by adding the hot milks in a very slow stream, whisking constantly. Stir in the cooked rice, the drained raisins, and almond extract.

Divide the mixture among the six ramekins. Place the ramekins in a bain-marie (a pan large enough to hold the ramekins in one layer with about an inch of hot water coming up their sides). Carefully transfer the pan to the oven and bake for 50 to 60 minutes, or just until a skewer inserted into the center of the puddings comes out clean. Let

cool for a half hour before unmold-
ing the puddings, or serve them
right in the ramekins. I prefer rice
pudding warm, but if you like it
cold, refrigerate, tightly covered
with plastic wrap, until chilled.

Options

➤ Plump the raisins in warm
  cognac to cover before using
  them.

➤ Sprinkle on a few teaspoons of
  toasted sweetened coconut
  flakes.

➤ Try this with leftover brown rice.

Crème Brûlée

Brûlée is classic, fairly easy to do, and offers an utterly addictive mouth-feel. I've upped the vanilla ante here, so if you don't adore vanilla, lower the amount used.

Makes 4 servings

1 pint heavy cream

1 vanilla bean (preferable) or

    1 teaspoon vanilla extract

¼ cup Superfine sugar

5 large egg yolks

Pinch of kosher salt

4 6-ounce heat- and flame-proof

    ramekins

Preheat oven to 325 degrees. Heat the cream in a medium saucepan over medium heat just until bubbles form on the sides of the pan.

In a medium bowl, gradually whisk the sugar into the egg yolks. Temper the yolks by slowly adding the hot cream to the yolk mixture, a few tablespoons at a time, whisking constantly. Strain the mixture through a fine sieve into a glass measure with a pouring spout. Stir in the salt.

Arrange the ramekins, not touching, in a deep baking pan. Pour the custard mixture into the ramekins. Fill the baking dish with hot tap water halfway up the sides of the ramekins, then cover the pan with foil.

Bake until just set, 25 to 35 minutes. The custard should wobble like Jell-O, but not be soupy. Remove pan from oven and let the ramekins cool, uncovered, in the water bath. Cover each ramekin with plastic wrap, and refrigerate at least 2 hours.

Return the custards to room temperature. Sift a thin, even layer of sugar over the custards. Ignite a blowtorch according to the manufacturer's instructions, and with a slow, sweeping motion, guide the flame around the surface of the custard. The nozzle should be 2 to 3 inches from the surface. The sugar will melt slowly at first, then caramelize quickly. When the entire surface is a glossy mahogany, go to the next custard. If you don't have a blowtorch, caramelize under a broiler. Serve at once.

Orange Zesty Ice Cream

This is more of a dessert for grown-ups, because it's not quite as sweet as most ice creams. It has a backdrop of spices and bittersweet orange zest, and it has a bit of liquor in it. I like to make it even *more* grown-up by pouring more Cointreau over it when I serve it.

Makes 1½ quarts

4 extra-large egg yolks

⅔ cup sugar

1 cup milk

½ teaspoon ground mace

½ teaspoon cinnamon

3 cups heavy cream

2 tablespoons best quality vanilla extract

½ teaspoon salt

2 tablespoons Cointreau, plus additional for serving (optional)

Zest of 2 medium organic oranges, cut into ⅛- by 1-inch strips

In a large heavy saucepan, whisk the egg yolks for 30 seconds, until pale yellow. Gradually whisk in the sugar and continue whisking until the mixture is lighter in color and forms a ribbon when you lift the whisk, about 2 minutes.

Whisk in the milk, mace, and cinnamon, and place the saucepan over moderately low heat. Cook, stirring often with a wooden spoon, until just hot, 3 to 5 minutes. Reduce the heat slightly and continue to cook, stirring constantly and watchfully, scraping the bottom of the pot to prevent scalding, until the custard thickens noticeably but does not curdle, 5 to 7 minutes longer.

Strain the mixture into a bowl, preferably stainless steel, and whisk in the cold cream, vanilla, salt, and Cointreau. Stir in the orange zest. Place the bottom of the bowl in a larger bowl of cold water. Cover the custard bowl and refrigerate until completely cold, at least 6 hours overnight.

Freeze the mixture according to your machine's manufacturer's directions. Pack into a covered container and freeze until just firm, 30 to 60 minutes. Pour a few tablespoons of Cointreau over each serving, and if you wish, ignite the liqueur with a very long match.

Chocolate, Hazelnut, and Honey Semifreddo

This frozen dessert is so simple it doesn't even require an ice-cream maker.

Makes 4 to 6 servings

7 egg yolks

1 cup honey

2 tablespoons warm water

1 cup melted dark chocolate

2 tablespoons hazelnut oil, or hazelnut liqueur like Frangelico

2 cups heavy cream, whipped until soft peaks form

¼ cup chopped toasted hazelnuts (optional)

In a standing electric mixer or hand-held mixer, beat the yolks with the honey until well combined and pale. Stir half the egg-honey mixture (with 2 tablespoons warm water added) into the melted chocolate and the oil or liqueur. When the mixture is well incorporated, stir in the remaining egg mixture. Finally, fold in the whipped cream and optional nuts until just combined. Pour the mixture into a 1-quart container, cover, and freeze the mixture overnight.

A Glossary of Asian Ingredients

Any worthwhile chef will agree that one of the most wonderful things about cooking is that you never stop learning. Even thrice-familiar ingredients have their secrets. And new food combination possibilities are endless.

To get the most out of this book, you might want to familiarize yourself with some ingredients you may never have worked with before. Some of these ingredients are used in this book; others I hope will inspire you to experiment with new flavors and substitutions in your favorite recipes. This ingredient glossary will acquaint you with Asian and Indian ingredients, from Achar to Yuzu. Then I've created A Spice Glossary and a collection of Fish Facts, which is followed by a brief explanation of various Japanese Cooking Terms. Finally, at the end of this section, I've provided several Internet sources for

ingredients that are scarcely encountered in most of America.

A

Achar (Acar, achard): The Indian name for pickled or salted vegetables.

Agar-agar: The Malay name for a gum extraction from red seaweed (genus *Eucheuma* and genus *Gelidium*). This gum is known as *kanten* in Japan, and it is a form of vegetable gelatin. It is used throughout Asia as a thickener, emulsifier, and stabilizer of many products.

Aioli: Garlic mayonnaise.

Amaranth: A leafy green commonly used in Southeast Asia, sometimes known as Chinese spinach. Some species also produce the grain amaranth.

Amchur or **Amchoor:** See A Spice Glossary.

Anardana: Dried seed of the pomegranate, used in the same way as amchur.

Anchovy: A family of fish found in all the warm oceans and used throughout the world. In the Mediterranean it is salted, then sold in barrels, although today it is more familiar in cans. It imparts a distinctive, salty flavor to many dishes. In Asia, it is usually dried or made into fish sauce.

Azuki or **Adzuki beans:** Small, red beans which have long been cultivated in Asia. This bean is tender with a mild, sweet flavor and is used predominantly in dessert fillings.

B

Bamboo: A member of the grass family whose very young shoots are harvested just as they appear above the ground. These tender shoots are a popular vegetable throughout Asia.

Banana flower: Sometimes known as banana heart, this flower is used in many Asian cultures, especially in Thailand, Laos, and Vietnam. The flower (technically the male part of the flower) is sheathed in reddish outer petals, which are removed. The pale inner heart is cooked into curries or sliced for salads. The banana flower is not particularly flavorful (don't expect it to taste like bananas), but is used predominantly for texture.

Banana leaf: The large leaf of a banana plant is generally used to wrap food before grilling or roasting. The leaf itself is not eaten, but it does impart a floral, herbacious flavor to food.

Basil: An aromatic herb native to India, Southeast Asia, and now commonly used throughout the Mediterranean. There are various species: Holy basil is commonly used in Southeast Asia and has a distinct clovelike fragrance, and Thai basil generally has purple stems and green leaves with a heavy aniseed or licorice flavor. The basil that we commonly use has a mild anise flavor and is slightly more floral.

Bean sprouts: These are produced by allowing seeds to germinate and grow for a short time, just long enough to produce shoots. The Chinese use mung bean sprouts as well as soybean sprouts. These are highly nutritious because during the sprouting process some of the starch and proteins in the seeds break down, making them more digestable.

Belachan: The Malay name for fermented shrimp paste. It is known as *terasi* in Indonesia, *kapi* in Thailand, and *bagoong* in the Philippines. Belachan is always cooked and ground with spices and chilies.

Bento: A Japanese term applied to small dishes which go into a specially prepared lunch box. The contents of the box may range from very simple to complex and expensive. Rice is usually a component, to-gether with the accompaniments, which may include pickles, fish, and or a small salad.

Bergamot: An herb in the mint family. Not related to the bergamot orange, whose oil is extracted and used to flavor Earl Grey tea.

Besan flour: Chickpea flour, sometimes also known as gram flour. It is a basic in-gredient in Indian cooking. It is made by milling chickpeas. The pale yellow flour is very high in protein content. Chickpea flour is also used in making *panisse*, as well as *socca* (both specialties of Provence).

Biriani: A term of Persian origin, meaning fried. It generally refers to a spicy dish of basmati rice and braised meat seasoned with saffron.

Bitter gourd or **bitter melon:** This veg-etable is neither a gourd nor a melon. The knobby fruit has a bitter taste and is used throughout Asia, where it is considered a delicacy.

Black beans (fermented): Salted, dried soybeans. In most processes the raw beans are salted and allowed to soften with their enzymes at high temperatures. The action of the enzymes darkens the beans, which are then salted, dried, and packed. Black beans have a highly salty and pungent flavor. I think they taste a lit-tle like Moroccan oil–cured olives.

Bok choy or **bok choi** or **pak choi:** A transliteration from Chinese. The bok choy is a cabbage with white stems and dark green leaves.

Borage: A plant common in northern Eu-rope and the Mediterranean with very pretty blue flowers and hairy leaves and a distinct cucumber flavor. The young leaves are used in salads, while the flowers may be used as a garnish.

Brittle: A hard confection usually made from sugar syrup cooked to the caramel stage and poured over nuts. Sesame and peanut brittles are commonly used in Asia.

Buckwheat: A member of the rhubarb family, the grain is either eaten whole as kasha or ground up into flour. Buckwheat flour is made into soba noodles and is also incorporated into batters for blini.

Burdock: A plant from the daisy family, burdock is eaten on a large scale in Japan, where it is called *gobo*. The root is thick, short, and hollow inside. Burdock resem-bles salsify, but it is slightly bitter.

C

Calamansi or **Kalamansi:** A hybrid of the mandarin orange and the kumquat. This fruit looks like a small mandarin orange, and is very acidic with slight orange over-tones and some spice.

Candlenut: An edible nut cultivated in India and Southeast Asia. It is a hard, wrinkly nut which is not eaten raw because it contains a toxin that must be cooked out. Candlenuts have an oily texture and nutty flavor when cooked. Macadamia nuts are usually substituted.

Carambola (star fruit): A small tree which bears an elongated yellow-green fruit with five prominent ridges running down it so that when cut it is star-shaped. The fruit itself is quite bland, a little like a very mild watermelon or slightly sweet cucumber. Carambola thrives in Caribbean countries, Hawaii, Central and South America, and parts of Asia.

Ceviche: A specialty of Central and South America, ceviche consists of raw fish marinated in lime or lemon juice or other acid and served as an appetizer. The acid in the juice cooks the protein in the fish. In the Philippines, there is a variation of the ceviche known as *kinilaw*.

Chapati: An unleavened flat circular bread which originates from the Indian subcontinent. It is made with whole-wheat flour and water, rolled very thin, and cooked without fat on a curved griddle called a *tava*. Most Indian flat breads are generally lumped under the generic term *roti*, which just means bread.

Chervil: A leafy herb which looks like a more feathery, delicate parsley. Chervil has a light, mild flavor between that of parsley and anise or licorice.

Chickpea: A legume first grown in ancient Egypt and the Middle East, but now extensively used throughout the world. Chickpeas are almost always sold in dried form, although for a short period during the spring in countries like Italy and parts of Spain it is possible to find fresh chickpeas. Finely milled chickpea flour is used for *panisse* (a kind of polenta made with chickpea flour) and for making batters.

Chinese chive or **garlic chive:** Unlike the common onion chive, Chinese chives are more closely related to the garlic chive. The name chive has stuck because it closely resembles the common chive. The leaf of the Chinese chive tends to be bigger, flatter, and solid rather than hollow in cross section, with a distinct garliclike flavor. There are two main varieties: The large Chinese chive is grown mainly for its leaves and is used as a vegetable, while the smaller chive is grown for its white blossom, which is used as a garnish as well as a vegetable. For our purposes, the smaller chives are known as chive buds.

Chinese water chestnut: It's not really a nut, but rather an underground stem known as a corm. It is used mainly to add texture to food and is a source of starch commonly used in Chinese cooking, especially Cantonese.

Chinese wolfberry: A berry from a small shrub sometimes known as the boxthorn. The berry is small and red, with a slightly sweet flavor. It is used most commonly because it has a reputation as a tonic. The Chinese name for them means "drive-away-old-age berry."

Chrysanthemum: In the Western world, this plant is a source of blossoms; however, in Asia, mainly Japan, China, and Korea, the leaves and young shoots are cooked as a green vegetable (known in the United States primarily by its Japanese name *shungiku*, which is also what dandelion leaves are called). The blossoms are also made into chrysanthemum tea.

Chutney: Derived from an Indian word meaning spicy relish. In America, chutney usually refers to a condiment consisting of fruit cooked with sugar and vinegar. The words chutney and relish are used almost interchangeably, but the main difference is that chutney consists of cooked fruit or vegetables, whereas relish consists of raw ingredients. In essence, relish is closer to what we now call salsa.

Coconut cream: Not to be confused with cream of coconut, such as Coco Lopez's sweetened mixture. The top-third of an *unshaken* can of unsweetened coconut milk will usually have a thicker cream that has separated from the milk below it. Spoon that out when coconut cream is called for in my recipes.

Congee: A watery porridge or gruel made with rice. Think of it as a form of Asian bisque without the cream.

Curry powder: A spice mixture which is likely to include coriander, cumin, mustard seeds, black pepper, fenugreek, turmeric, cinnamon, cardamom, and cayenne. Curry powders differ from region to region depending on the quantity of heat (cayenne) used in the mixture.

Cuttlefish: A cephalopod commonly used in Asia, cuttlefish is not dissimilar to the squid, only larger and slightly meatier.

D

Daikon: A slightly sweet, crunchy, large Japanese radish.

Dal: Indian name for lentils, or dried pulses.

Dashi: A soup stock that is made with dried bonito tuna flakes (*katsuobushi*), *kombu* (a sun-dried seaweed), and water.

Dim sum: An important institution of Cantonese cuisine, it literally translates as "touch the heart." Dim sum is in reality a large array of hors d'oeuvres consisting of dumplings which may be steamed, fried, or boiled, as well as roasted meats. Think of it as Asian tapas.

Dosa: A South Indian pancake, crispy on the surface, but spongy inside with a faintly sour taste because the batter is slightly fermented, not unlike sourdough bread.

Dulse: The most widely distributed of the edible red seaweeds from the Indo-Pacific to the Atlantic. These plants have a lightly salty taste.

E

Enokitake or **Enoki:** A mushroom with long thin stems and small yellow to orange-brown caps. Enokis grow in clusters and are commonly used in stews and soups.

Escabache: A preparation of fish which is fried, cooled, and then marinated in a hot mixture of vinegar and other ingredients. This dish is generally served cold. Common in Mediterranean cooking.

F

Farina: A word of Latin derivation that in both English and Italian means flour. In my restaurants, we used the word farina to mean cream of wheat.

Fish sauce: An essential part of Southeast Asian cooking, fish sauce is made by fermenting small, whole fish in vats of brine and drawing off the liquid, which is then matured and bottled. Fish sauce keeps indefinitely.

Five spice: A Chinese ground spice mixture consisting generally of star anise, fennel, cloves, cinnamon, and Sichuan pepper. My own recipe appears on page 52.

G

Ghee: Clarified butter made from cow's milk, commonly used in India.

Ginkgo nut: A buff-colored nut enclosing a pale yellow kernel, which becomes pale green when cooked. Used in Chinese and Japanese cuisine, the kernel has a pleasant, mildly nutty taste.

Ginseng: A root which is thought to have medicinal as well as aphrodisiac properties. It is mildly bitter and quite pungent.

Goa: A region on the Southwest coast of India, Goan cuisine is greatly influenced by the Portuguese colonization of the area.

Golden Needle: A long thin dried bud of a lily which grows abundantly in northern China. These buds are used in stir-fried and steamed dishes. They have a delicately floral, slightly tangy flavor.

Gram: An Indian term referring to leguminous seeds called pulses which are whole rather than split. Split pulses are known as Dal.

H

Harissa: A condiment made from a paste of chile peppers used in North Africa. It also applies to a dish consisting of seared green peppers, tomatoes, and onions, which are peeled, pounded, and flavored with coriander, caraway, and garlic.

Harusame: A Japanese term meaning spring rain, referring to the appearance of a vermicelli-like product made either from mung bean, soybean, or corn flour. Harusame are commonly chopped and used to batter tempura.

Hen-of-the-Woods (called **mai-take** in Japan): An edible fungus with numerous caps that grows in clusters reminiscent of a hen's feather. The Japanese name, *mai-take*, means dancing mushroom. It is a mild, slightly woodsy mushroom with a slight bitter aftertaste.

Hijiki: One of the dried brown seaweeds that has a nutlike flavor and a crisp texture.

Hoja santa: A native of Central America, *hoja santa* is a plant with large anise- or sassafras-flavored leaves. It is used to wrap other foods.

I

Idli: A specialty of Southern India, *idli* are small dumplings made from a dough of ground rice and dal that is allowed to fer-ment overnight. Idli are steamed in a special pan and generally eaten with coconut chutney.

J

Jambu or **rose apple:** A fruit indigenous to Malaysia and Indonesia, the jambu is a cousin of the cashew nut. The flesh of the fruit tastes surprisingly like a mixture of a carambola, a cucumber, and a green apple.

Jellyfish: Highly valued in Asia, these are the strips taken from the dried umbrella part of the jellyfish. It is prized because of its texture, which is described as tender, crunchy, and elastic and is generally served with salads.

K

Kachori: Stuffed *poori*, similar to samosa; these dumplings are an important part of Indian street foods.

Kaffir Lime: A member of the citrus family that is important to Southeast Asian cuisine. The fruit is knobby and bitter and is sometimes used for its juice. The leaves of the plant are a more common ingredient, imparting a delightfully citric, spicy, and bright flavor. In some respects, kaffir lime leaves are used in the way that bay leaves are used in Europe.

Katsuobushi or **Bonito Flakes:** Dried fillets of the skipjack that are shaved. An integral part of dashi.

Kecap Manis: A thickened, sweetened soy sauce.

Khichri: A popular Indian dish of rice and lentils with spices. It is the origin of a dish known as kedgeree, which is part of the Anglo-Indian cooking tradition.

Kibbeh: A paste of grain (bulgur wheat), meat, and onions that is formed into patties and fried. *Kibbeh* is not always cooked, and sometimes resembles a tartare.

Kimchi or **Kimchee:** A fermented vegetable relish that is one of the most important foods of Korea. It is generally served as an accompaniment for rice. Typical vegetables used for kimchi include cabbage, daikon, cucumber, leeks, and lots and lots of garlic and chile peppers.

Kinilaw: A dish from the Philippines that is similar to a ceviche. It refers to fresh, uncooked fish marinated in vinegar or lime juice.

Kochojang: A paste of fermented chile pepper and soybeans from Korea that is used to add flavor to savory dishes.

Kombu: The general name for many of the large brown seaweeds, kombu is found in dashi and many stews and is rich in natural MSG.

Korma: In India and Pakistan, korma refers to a dish that is braised or stewed, often enriched with ground nuts and yogurt.

Krupuk: Malay name for a thin, savory cracker. The basic dough is made by mixing flour (wheat, cassava, rice, or a mixture of all of them) with other ingredients to provide flavor. It is then rolled into logs, steamed, sliced, and dried in the sun to make a thin, dense, exceedingly hard biscuit. When fried in hot oil, it doubles in size and becomes crunchy. The most popular form of *krupuk* are prawn crackers.

Kumquat: A fruit resembling a miniature orange but that is not even a member of the citrus family. Kumquats have a golden rind that is soft, thin, and pulpy with very little pith, unlike that of a true citrus. The fruit can be eaten whole, although it is quite tart and sometimes bitter, with a spicy, citric flavor.

L

Laab: A Thai chopped meat salad.

Laksa: A term derived from the Persian word noodle. *Laksa* now refers solely to a Malaysian noodle broth rich with meat, fish, and coconut milk.

Lavash: A thin crisp bread usually made with flour, shaped in a variety of ways. Originating in the Caucasus Mountain region, lavash is leavened and baked in a tandoor, served with kebabs, and used to scoop up foods or wrapped around food before it is eaten.

Longan: A smaller, less flavorful member of the lychee family.

Loquat: A medium-sized tree of the rose family, the loquat's yellow-orange fruit is oval-shaped and tastes remarkably like an apricot or peach, to which it is related.

Lotus: An extraordinary plant that has edible leaves, root, and seeds. The young leaves can be cooked while the older, larger ones are used as wrapping for foods to be steamed. The root, which is actually a rhizome (a swollen underground stem), resembles large sausage links. The "links" are reddish-brown with internal tunnels. They have a crisp texture and a lacy pattern. Lotus root is sometimes ground into a paste and used as a thickener, or made into lotus flour. The seeds resemble shelled peanuts and have a mildly nutty flavor.

Lumpia: A Filipino spring roll.

Lychee: A fruit from a large tree grown in southern China and Southeast Asia, the lychee is a round fruit with a tough, knobby skin which turns red when the fruit is ripe. Inside is a delicate, white pulp surrounding a single, shiny dark brown seed. Its flavor is a cross between a Muscat grape and a mild mango. When dried the lychee develops a molasseslike flavor a little like a chewy date.

M

Mandarin: A small, loose-skinned orange fruit. Satsumas, clementines, and tangerines are all types of mandarins. Tangelos are a hybrid between a mandarin and a pomelo or a grapefruit.

Mango: One of the most popular tropical fruits, there are hundreds of varieties of mangoes. The fruits vary in length and shape from round to long and narrow. They generally have a yellow-green or orange color with a red flush. Mangoes have a large stone covered with fibers and a highly aromatic, meaty, juicy flesh. Some common varieties are the Alphonso, Hayden, and Manila. The unripe fruit is used extensively in Southeast Asia for making chutneys and pickles, as well as in salads.

Masala: A spice mixture from India, the best-known masala is Garam Masala (page 55; garam meaning hot), which includes cardamom, cumin, cloves, black pepper, cinnamon, and coriander. Blends of masala vary enormously according to regional tastes. *Chaat* masala is a tart and salty spice blend which gets its unique taste from *amchur; Gujerati* masala is another hot spice mixture with the addition of dried chilies, fennel seeds, and onion seeds; while *kashmiri* masala is dominated by cardamom. *Taaza* masala is a green spice paste based on cilantro, mint, garlic, and ginger, while *shakuti* masala is a speciality of Goa consisting of coriander, cumin, black pepper, fenugreek, and chilies, all blended with roasted coconut to give it a toasted nutty taste.

Matsutake: Japanese for pine mushrooms, it is a large meaty mushroom which has a very fragrant, distinct, piney flavor.

Mioga ginger: A close relation of gingerroot that is valued for its buds. The buds are very fragrant like gingerroot, but not as hot. They are often used in salads, pickles, and as a garnish on foods.

Mirin: Sweetened rice wine.

Miso: Fermented paste of soybeans and either rice or barley. Miso comes in different colors; the color difference is due to the different ingredients that the miso is made from: *komemiso*—rice and soybeans, *mugimiso*—barley and soybeans, and *mamemiso*—soybeans alone, as well as its method of fermentation. Pale miso (also called white or blond miso) is milder and fermented for less time, while dark miso is fermented longer. In China, miso is known as *dou jiang*. Miso is fermented in two stages. First a mold (*Aspergillus oryzae*) is grown on steamed grain, either rice or barley. This forms a *koju* (starter). Soybeans are soaked, steamed, and mixed with the

koju together with salt and water. The mixture is allowed to ferment, forming miso.

Mung bean: The seed of a plant that is native to India, but is now widespread throughout Asia. The two most common uses for the bean are to make bean sprouts and as a source of starch for mung bean noodles.

N

Nam prik: A popular sauce in Thailand consisting of chopped red chile, fish sauce, lime juice, garlic, and a little sugar.

Nori: Made from laver, an important group of seaweed, nori in Japan is sold in paper-thin sheets called *honshi-nori*.

O

Octopus: A member of the mollusk family, octopus is very popular in the Mediterranean and Asia. The meat of the octopus (mostly from the tentacles) is very dense, mild, and sweet. There is quite a lot of folklore surrounding the cooking and tenderizing of octopus, including adding a cork to the cooking liquid, or beating the octopus on rocks.

Okra: An annual plant that bears a pod that is typically ridged and tapered, containing many small seeds. Okra has a gummy texture when cooked, and a slimy texture if it's overcooked. It has a mild flavor and is very popular in Indian cooking.

Opah: A large and beautiful fish with pink, firm flesh and fairly mild, almost meaty flavor.

Oyster Mushrooms: Oyster mushrooms look a little like traditional white mushrooms and have a slippery texture. They are either white or gray, with a slightly peppery flavor.

P

Pakora: A batter-fried vegetable from India or Pakistan, usually eaten as a snack. The batter is frequently made with chickpea flour flavored with coriander, turmeric, and cayenne.

Palm Sugar: Called jaggery or *gula malaka* or *gula java*, palm sugar is obtained from the sap of the palmyra palm and is widely used in Southeast Asia. Palm sugar is dark brown, crumbly, tasting of slightly smoky molasses.

Panch Phoron: Persian five-spice powder consisting of mustard seed, cumin, fenugreek, nigella seeds, and fennel. It is the distinctive spice of the state of Bengal and is used to flavor pulses and vegetables.

Panir or **paneer:** Fresh cheese from the Middle East and India.

Papaya: A pear-shaped tropical fruit. The ripe papaya is yellow or orange. A creamy, sweet, delicately scented fruit, papayas have little to no acidity. Unripe papaya is used in salads in Southeast Asia.

Paratha: Flaky Indian bread prepared by smearing the unleavened and enriched dough with ghee. The dough is folded over a few times then fried, and the resulting bread is flaky and separates into layers.

Pear: Like apples, pears belong to the rose family. Some of the more common varieties include Anjou (called *beurre* in some countries), a soft and juicy variety with a slightly gritty texture, tapered, with a yellowish-green, russet skin; Bosc, closely related to the Anjou, but a little firmer, with a long, tapered neck; Bartlett (also called Williams), a meaty, juicy pear with a mild musky flavor; Comice, a broad, green pear with a red blush particularly sweet and aromatic; Seckel, an American variety, a hard, spicy pear with a gritty texture. Asian Pears are more closely related to a wild pear. They tend to be "apple-shaped" with a brownish-yellow skin, and are sometimes called *nishi* or Harbin pears.

Peking duck: A term used to describe a special way of cooking duck. The duck is killed and plucked, then air is pumped between the skin and body so that the bird is inflated. It is blanched in boiling water and coated with maltose, and allowed to dry. Finally the bird is roasted in a special vertical oven where the ducks are hung so that the fat drips off while they are being cooked. As a result, the duck has a shiny, crisp skin and succulent flesh. It is usually served with pancakes, scallions, and a sweet bean paste.

Persimmon: There are two main varieties of persimmon: the *fuju*, which is a flat, apple-shaped fruit that is hard, with a tough, almost leathery skin. Its flesh is orange, sweet, and mildly flavored. This variety is the American persimmon, which is common during the fall and winter. It is made into puddings or dried. The hachiya persimmon is larger, and more peach-shaped. This variety becomes soft as it ripens, and is best eaten ripe as it is quite tannic when green. The flesh of this variety is creamy, more fragrant, and is more popular in Asia.

Pilaf or **pilau:** The Middle-Eastern and Indian method of cooking rice and bulgur as well as a dish of rice. The rice is flavored with spices like cardamom, cinnamon, and sometimes saffron, and served to accompany curries or stews.

Pomegranate: The fruit of a small tree, pomegranates are laborious to consume. The pulp that surrounds hundreds of tiny, ruby-like seeds are separated by a thin membrane, making it difficult to extract. The pulp itself is sweet-tart and has a very distinctive flavor. Pomegranates are popu-

lar throughout Asia. When juiced, it makes a refreshing drink, which can be reduced to a syrup (pomegranate molasses). Grenadine is made from pomegranates.

Ponzu: A Japanese dipping sauce consisting of citrus juice (yuzu in particular; see page 190) and soy sauce.

Poori: An Indian flat bread which puffs up when it's deep-fried. *Poori* is sometimes filled with lentils, herbs, and potatoes.

Poppadom: Thin crisp bread sometimes referred to as a wafer. When fried it becomes crisp and crunchy. It is usually flavored with spices like dried chilies and black peppercorn.

Prawn cracker: See krupuk.

R

Rambutans: A native fruit of Malaysia, rambutans are closely related to the lychee. The fruit ranges from green to red, the inside looks and tastes like a lychee, while the outside is covered with long hairs.

Rau ram: An herb commonly called Vietnamese coriander, *rau ram* has narrow, pointed leaves that have a coriander/mint/basil-like flavor.

Red cook: A term that refers to a Chinese method of cooking in which the meat is braised in soy sauce and other seasonings.

Rendang: A dish from Malaysia and Western Sumatra consisting of beef that is stewed with shallots, ginger, turmeric, and coconut milk. Unlike regular stews, the braising liquid is reduced until it forms a thick paste.

Rose apple: See jambu.

Roti: A general Indian term for a flat bread roasted at high heat.

S

Sago: A light starch obtained from the stems of various palms. It is formed into round pallets similar to tapioca, just slightly less starchy and more translucent when cooked.

Sake: Japanese rice wine.

Salsify: *Scolymus* or *schorzonera*, a root that is popular in Italy and France, as well as Japan. The root of the salsify resembles a long, white carrot and is usually baked, boiled, or sautéed. Pickled salsify is popular in Japan and Korea.

Salt cod: Cod that has been salted and dried. Salt cod is the most common variety of dried fish in the West. There are numerous varieties of salted and dried fish throughout Asia.

Sambal: A Malay word for a wide range of condiments, mostly hot and spicy. The term is now specifically applied to a hot chile condiment.

Samosa: A small, crisp, flaky pastry made in India. Stuffed with a variety of fillings such as cheese, meat, and vegetables, it is usually fried but sometimes baked.

Samshire or **sea beans:** A plant found near the sea, particularly around estuaries. As a result the plant is quite briny and tastes like the sea.

Satay or **saté:** A Southeast Asian dish consisting of small strips of meat, chicken, or fish threaded onto skewers and grilled. Marinades vary from place to place, the common accompaniment for satay is a dipping sauce made of peanuts.

Sauerkraut: Because of its German name, we normally associate sauerkraut with the cuisine of Germany, when in reality the Chinese are believed to be the first to have made it. Thinly sliced cabbage is packed in a crock with salt; it is then covered and pressed down. This extracts the juice from the cabbage and excludes air, for the fermentation of sauerkraut is anaerobic (airless). Lactic bacteria naturally present in cabbage begin to ferment the sugar in the extracted liquid, causing it to sour.

Screwpine: Often called *pandanus*, screwpine is a grass commonly used for flavoring in Asia. It is the vanilla of Asia, where it is prized not just for its delicate flavor but also for the natural green color which can be obtained from its leaves by boiling them.

Sea urchin: *Uni* in Japanese, the sea urchin is a round creature with spines sticking out in all directions from its shell. Inside are five edible orange- or rose-colored ovaries known as coral.

Seaweed: A marine algae which is consumed in many countries, but is most closely associated with Japan. There are three main groups: the green and blue-green seaweed (sea lettuce and *awonori* are the most important); brown seaweed (which includes kombu and wakame); and red seaweed (nori, laver, *tengusa*, and dulse are the most common). Seaweed is generally processed by drying. Besides being consumed fresh, it is used to extract a stabilizer called agar-agar, which is used in Asian jellies.

Sesame Salt: Sea salt combined with lightly toasted white or black sesame seeds and ground.

Sev: An Indian noodle made from chick-pea flour.

Shark's fin: This is obviously the fin of a shark; it is highly prized in China and Japan. The fins are sold dried. The cartilaginous "strands" of the fin are gelatinous and are thought to be an aphrodisiac.

Shichimi: A Japanese spice mixture. The name means seven flavors, which are red chili flakes, sanso, white poppy seeds, white sesame seeds, rape seeds, mandarin orange or yuzu peel, and nori.

Shiitake: A meaty mushroom commonly used in Japan and China. The shiitake is mildly woody and earthy. Dried shiitakes (also called dried Chinese mushrooms and black mushrooms) have quite an intense flavor that is slightly smoky.

Shiso: Also called perilla, this herb is a member of the mint family. Its large leaves are used for wrapping certain foods as well as for flavoring. The purple variety is sometimes used for coloring *umeboshi* plums and ginger a faint pink. Its flavor is peppermintlike with hints of cumin.

Sichuan mustard (also spelled **Szechuan**): The preserved tuber from the mustard plant. It is sometimes rubbed with a little chile paste. The plump vegetable is crisp in texture, salty, sour, and spicy in taste.

Sinigang: A sour Filipino stew, similar to soups like the Thai *tom yam* or the Malaysian *asam laksa*.

Soba: Japanese word for buckwheat and for the noodles made from buckwheat.

Somen: Japanese noodle made from wheat.

Soybeans: *Edamame*, a legume that is really high in protein (35 percent), far beyond that of any plant. Fresh beans are eaten as a snack and have a mildly nutty, green flavor. Dried soybeans are used in products like tofu and soy milk, as well as miso and tempe.

Soy sauce: The universal condiment of Asia. Made by fermenting soybeans and rice to develop a paste (miso) and a liquid (*shoyu* or soy sauce).

Sweet potato: A tropical root crop, sweet potatoes are members of the morning glory family and are not related to the potato.

T

Tabbouleh: Traditionally a salad made from parsley, diced tomato, and cracked wheat (bulgur), tossed with lemon juice and olive oil.

Tahini: A paste made of sesame seeds.

Tamarillo or **tree tomato:** A subtropical fruit that grows in bushes and resembles a tomato. The fruit is reddish or yellow surrounding small black seeds. Its flavor is a cross between that of a tomato and a mango, with a sweet-tart taste.

Tamarind: A fruit from a tropical tree. Tamarind is prized for its pods, which grow in clusters containing small seeds surrounded by a sweet-sour pulp. The pulp or paste is used as flavoring. Tamarind has a strong sweet-tart taste, with a background

flavor that is similar to that of most dried fruit (molasseslike and slightly caramel).

Tandoor: A conical oven built of clay that is common in India, Pakistan, and parts of the Middle East. Any food cooked in a tandoor is known as tandoori.

Tapioca: A starchy extraction from the cassava, which is a tropical root. The extraction is formed into pearls, which we know as tapioca.

Taro: Another tropical root, taro is an important food source. It is large and white with purple veins running through it. The flavor of taro is slightly earthier than that of a regular potato.

Tempura: A Japanese name given to fish or vegetables fried in a light batter.

Tikka: A Hindi word for skewers or kebab.

Tofu: White curd made from soybean milk. Fermented tofu is very pungent because it's made by fermenting fresh tofu with rice or barley. Tofu skins are thin sheets of dried tofu, generally used as a wrapper, but sometimes just sliced and added to soups or stews without a filling.

U

Udon: Japanese wheat noodles.

Umeboshi: Salted and dried Japanese "plums." They are typically purple because they are usually pickled with dark red shiso leaves.

V

Vietnamese Mint Leaves: These are grown in two varieties: spicy (*rau ram*) and mildly minty (*rau hung*). The flavor of the latter, which is preferred, is very close to spearmint.

Vindaloo: A stew from Goa, which is on the southwest coast of India, where the cuisine was strongly influenced by the Portuguese, who colonized the region. Vindaloo is a vinegary and spicy stew redolent of coriander, cardamom, and ginger.

W

Water Spinach: Also known as swamp cabbage or *kangkong*, water spinach is a plant that grows in water and is common throughout Asia. When cooked, the stems remain crisp while the leaves take on a silky quality.

Wheat products: Bulgur—cracked wheat, when the wheat is partially boiled, parched, and coarsely ground.

Winged bean: A tropical legume whose pods have four wavy ridges running along them. They are sometimes called asparagus beans because they are thought to taste like asparagus.

Wonton: A savory Chinese dumpling. Wontons may either be steamed, pan-fried, or deep-fried.

Wood-ear mushroom: A staple of Asian cooking, wood-ear mushrooms grow on trees. They have very little flavor and are usually added to dishes like hot-and-sour soup for texture.

Y

Yuba: The Japanese name for tofu skin. It is the delicate skin that forms on the surface of soy milk when it is heated. These skins are lifted off and dried.

Yuzu: A citrus that grows in China and Japan. The fruit is the size of a mandarin orange, bright yellow when ripe, with a thick uneven leaf and many pips. It tastes like a lime with a very sharp, slightly peppery flavor.

A Spice Glossary

Ajwain or **ajowan seeds:** Tiny seeds produced by an herb related to cumin, caraway, parsley, and dill. They have a fragrance similar to cumin with a more intense and assertive flavor with licorice and thyme overtones.

Aleppo pepper: The powder made from a Syrian chile. This is not a spicy chile, although it does have some heat. It is prized mostly for its smoky, sweet flavor.

Allspice: Whole dried, unripe berries of a large evergreen tree, a member of the myrtle family. The berries are dark, reddish-brown, with a strong fragrance similar to clove. Allspice combines the characteristic flavors of clove, nutmeg, pepper, and cinnamon.

Amchoor powder: A powder made by grinding sun-dried green mangoes. It is used extensively in Indian pickles, as well as a source of acidity.

Anise: These are oval, aromatic seeds from an herb closely related to cumin and fennel. It has a bittersweet, strong, fruity flavor with hints of licorice.

Annatto seeds: The brick-red seeds and pods of a small evergreen tree. The seeds are ground into a paste and used for coloring. It has a faintly peppery nutmeg flavor and is mostly prized because it imparts color to food with barely discernible flavor.

Bay leaf: The aromatic, green leaf from the sweet bay tree native to the Mediterranean. The leaf has a mildly peppery, citrus, and woodsy flavor. Fresh California bay leaves are quite fragrant.

Betel leaf: Not to be confused with betel nut (which is the nut of the areca palm), Betel leaves are generally eaten raw and used as a wrapping for food in India and Thailand. Betel leaves are related to the pepper vine and taste a lot like a very strong arugula.

Black bean: Technically not a spice, black beans are the dried, fermented, and salted steamed soybeans. They have a slightly musty, intense flavor.

Black salt: Used in northern India, black salt is sold in crystal or powder form. Black salt is mined from quarries found in central India. In actual fact, black salt contains no sodium and has a more interesting flavor and smell than taste.

Caper: The caper is the unopened flower bud of the caper bush. The bud is hand-picked, salted or pickled, and used as a condiment.

Caraway seeds: Seeds from the caraway plant, a member of the parsley family. They have a warm, nutty flavor with a hint of licorice.

Cardamom: The small green pods of the cardamom plant, a member of the ginger family. The seeds have a sweet, camphorlike fragrance. Cardamom is an important component of Garam Masala.

Cassia: The bark of the camphor-laurel tree, commonly found in Indian, Chinese, Thai, Vietnamese, and other Southeast Asian cuisine. Cassia is used interchangeably with cinnamon, but its flavor is less delicate.

Cinnamon: The soft inner bark of the cinnamon tree, a member of the camphor-laurel tree indigenous to Sri Lanka. Unlike cassia, cinnamon is rolled into tight quills. They have an aroma reminiscent of a tropical jungle (warm, sweet, and intense). Whole cinnamon quills are generally used for curries.

Clove: The dried flower of a member of the myrtle family with a powerful, slightly astringent, and sweetly pungent flavor. Cloves are often a component of Garam Masala as well as five-spice powder.

Coriander seeds: Seeds of the coriander plant that are related to both the parsley and carrot families. Coriander seeds have a clean, citrus, woody, and peppery flavor. The leaf of the coriander plant is commonly known as cilantro.

Cumin seeds: Cumin, a member of the parsley family with a distinctive strong aroma and a bittersweet, assertive, and warm, earthy flavor. Cumin is a component of Garam Masala.

Curry leaf: *Murraya koenigli*, a small tropical shrub native to India and Sri Lanka. These leaves have a powerful, citric, slightly curry flavor which dissipates on cooking.

Curry Powder: A spice mixture likley to include coriander, cumin, mustard seeds, black pepper, fenugreek, turmeric, cinnamon, cardamom, and cayenne. Curry powders differ from region to region depending on the quantity of heat (cayenne) used in the mixture.

Dried tangerine peel: Dried orange, mandarin, or tangerine peel may be used in Chinese dishes. It adds a subtle citrus flavor that is more haunting and less obvious than the flavor of fresh zest. Dried peels are usually used in stews with duck, pork, or lamb. It is thought to cut through the fat of these meats.

Galangal: A rhizome, and a member of the ginger family. Galangal resembles ginger in appearance, has a pinkish-red skin with creamy-white, slightly woody flesh. Galangal has a slightly more peppery, camphorlike flavor than ginger and is usually used in conjunction with ginger, especially in Southeast Asia.

Grains of paradise: The seeds of a reed-like herbaceous plant that is a member of the ginger family and is native to Western Africa. The seeds are peppery—very peppery—and spicy, with faint hints of cinnamon and camphor. They may be ground and used like pepper.

Juniper berry: Small purplish-blue berry of the cypress tree that is native to northern Europe. These berries are the main flavor component in gin.

Kokum (sometimes known as **bale fruit**): The dried rind of the purple-fleshed fruit of the kokum tree, used to impart a tart flavor, as well as a pinkish color to the foods with which it is cooked.

Lemongrass: An aromatic herb (grass actually) that is used in curries, particularly Thai curries. It has a clean, citric (some say citronella) flavor.

Mace: A large equatorial tree which produces an apricotlike fruit. The arial or seed covering of the fruit is known as mace, while the seed is known as nutmeg. Mace looks like a red lacy glove with a sweet, very pungent, yet slightly bitter flavor, much stronger and quite different from that of nutmeg.

Mustard seeds: Pungent, hot, and aromatic with an acrid, mustard flavor. Golden-yellow mustard seeds have a slightly nuttier flavor, while black mustard seeds are more pungent and fiery.

Nigella: The seed of the sativa, which is a common garden plant in the Mediterranean, with a slightly peppery-poppy seed and onionlike flavor.

Nutmeg: The seed of an equatorial tree with a sweet, warm flavor. See mace.

Papaya seeds: Papaya seeds are not normally used as a spice, but they have a really distinctive peppery flavor similar to that of the mustard cress. They also contain papain, an enzyme that breaks down meat fibers and is used primarily as a meat tenderizer.

Paprika: A fine red powder made by grinding dried mild chilies. I like to use Spanish paprika, which has a lovely smoky flavor and a rich red-orange color. Spanish paprika is available in mild, bittersweet, and hot formats.

Saffron: The stigma of a purple crocus, saffron is the most expensive spice in the world because the stigma has to be laboriously collected by hand. Saffron has a sweet, floral, complex aroma, and a slightly bitter flavor.

Sansho pepper: The dried, ground seed pods of a variety of prickly ash tree; it gives off a certain amount of heat and then has a slightly numbing effect on the tongue. It has mint, basil, and licorice overtones.

Sesame seeds: The seeds of a herbaceous tropical plant, the small, flat seeds have a high oil content and a nutty flavor that becomes really pronounced after the seeds are toasted.

Sichuan pepper: Also known as *fagara* or Chinese pepper, Sichuan pepper has a spicy, earthy flavor and produces a slightly numbing effect. It was recently banned in the United States because it sometimes carries cankers that attack citrus plants. But the ban was lifted—provided that the imported peppercorns have been heated to 140 degrees for 10 minutes to destroy the cankers.

Star anise: A staple in Chinese and Vietnamese cooking, this beautiful spice is the sun-dried fruit of a member of the magnolia family. The fruit, an eight-pointed star, has a delicate fragrance and a sweet licorice flavor.

Tamarind: Tamarind is produced from the pod of the tamarind tree. The pod contains seeds and a dark brown sticky pulp that is dried and used to impart tartness to food. It also has a fruity, sweet-tart flavor.

Turmeric: A rhizome related to the ginger family, turmeric is bright orange when fresh and golden yellow when dried. Its flavor is a little milder than that of regular ginger, slightly more peppery, and a little more bitter.

Vanilla bean: The pods of a fleshy tropical orchid. The beans are picked when immature and yellow, and sun-dried for several months, during which time they ferment and develop their familiar brown, wrinkled appearance and a rich, mellow, tobacco-like aroma. Each bean produces thousands of tiny, fragrant seeds, and an exotic, intense flavor.

Wasabi: The root of a mountain hollyhock, wasabi is totally unrelated to the European horseradish, although it is often called "Japanese horseradish." The root is pale green, fiery, and slightly nutty.

Fish Facts

Barramundi: A large fish with gray skin, barramundi is imported from Australia or New Zealand, where it is sometimes farmed. The flesh of the barramundi is firm, moist, and sweet, and is suitable for most cooking methods.

Char: A fish belonging to the salmon family with metallic blue-and-green backs and yellowish spots. Like salmon, its flesh is pink, oily, and very rich.

Dolphin (more commonly called **mahimahi**): So named because it has a hump on its head similar to a dolphin. A firm, mild white fish that is good for almost all forms of fish preparation.

Eel: The name applied to the fish of the genus *Anguilla*, which are born and die in the oceans, but spend most of their lives in fresh water. In Japan, eels have been farmed and eaten since antiquity. Eels are rich, mild, and firmly textured.

Grouper: Known in Southeast Asia as *kerapu*, these large fish are very firm and flaky with a mild flavor. There is a great deal of confusion about the fish, which is known by different names in different countries.

Gurnard: Commonly known as sea robin, this small fish is generally used in fish stews because its flesh is dry, but firm and white.

Haddock: A member of the cod family, with which haddock is sometimes used interchangeably. Like cod, it is a firm, mild white fish. Haddock is often sold smoked and salted.

Hake or **merluza:** Another member of the cod family, hake is highly prized in the Mediterranean. Like cod, it is a mild-tasting, firm white fish with large flakes.

Halibut: The largest of the flatfish, halibut is one of the more expensive fish on the market because its very rich flesh is prized for its pearly white color and firmness. Halibut is fished between April and November.

Jack: A general name used for an entire species of fish, which is almost always found in tropical or subtropical waters. The species includes mackerels and pompanos, as well as hamachi or yellowfin jack. Jacks are generally considered an oily fish.

John Dory: A fish from the Mediterranean and North Atlantic, with very mild thin fillets and small flakes.

Mackerel: A fish common in the North Atlantic and Mediterranean, a member of the Jack family. Mackerel have relatively high oil content and as a result taste quite fishy. The flesh is dense and dark. Mackerel is popular in both Mediterranean and Japanese cuisine.

Monkfish: Also called lotte or anglerfish, monkfish is an incredibly ugly fish with a large head and mouth and a tail, which is the only part that is sold. The flesh of the monkfish is firm and white and is often compared with that of a lobster. In fact, it was often referred to as the poor man's lobster until it became so popular it went up in price. Monkfish liver is considered to be a delicacy.

Pike: A freshwater fish that is mild and firm with flaky flesh. The common pike we use is the walleye pike from the lakes of the Midwest, where it is often called pickerel.

Ray or **skate:** The names are used interchangeably. Rays are a flatfish that lack true bones; rather, they have greatly enlarged pectoral fins, which is what we consume. The meat is sweet and white with a ropelike texture, although it is quite tender.

Red Mullet: Also known as rouget, red mullet is easily recognized for its bright red color and the tiny barbs around its mouth. This small fish never grows to be larger than 3 or 4 inches in length. It is prized for its firm, sweet flesh and very mild flavor.

Sea bass: One of the priciest fin fish, the flesh of the bass is fine-flavored and is relatively free of small bones. It is a firm fish that holds its shape well after it is cooked.

Sea bream or **daurade:** Very abundant in the Mediterranean, this oval fish is white, with fine flakes and a mild, sweet flavor.

Sea trout: An oily fish which is firm, meaty, and sweet. It is less commonly known as weakfish.

Snapper: Easily identified because of its pink color and bony head. Snappers are prized fish with sweet, white flesh and large flakes. There are various types of snapper, but the most popular is the American red. Snapper bones are excellent for making stock.

Sturgeon: One of the most primitive fish, sturgeon's roe is the source of caviar. There are about a dozen varieties. Some live at sea and spawn in fresh water, while others are purely freshwater. Most of the sturgeon we buy are farm-raised in Oregon and Washington state. The flesh of the sturgeon is firm, very meaty, and white. Its texture resembles that of a game fish (like tuna and swordfish).

Swordfish: A large game fish, there was a voluntary moratorium on swordfish over the past ten years because it had been overfished. You still don't see it on many menus, but it's somewhat more available. One of the best ways to cook swordfish is to cut it into steaks and grill it, because it has such compact, dense flesh.

Tautog: A member of the wrasse family, tautog is also called rock cod in the Northeast. It is a firm, white fish with large flakes and a very mild flavor.

Tilapia: A freshwater fish highly prized in Asia, tilapia is farmed in the United States. It is a white fish that is mild and sweet, but quite bony.

Tilefish: A deep-sea fish with brilliant colors, tilefish is a pretty inexpensive fish whose flesh is fine-grained with very good flavor.

Trout: There are many different varieties—golden, brown, brook, ocean, and rainbow, to name a few. The flesh of the trout varies from white to gray to pink, depending on its diet. Trout is a flaky, mild fish.

Tuna: Tuna is a game fish. There are a number of different species, but the best known is the yellowfin, which is the one most often used for sushi. Albacore tuna is sometimes known as white tuna, and they are caught during late summer and early fall when they are at their fattest. Tuna is pinky red-fleshed with a rich flavor and meaty texture. *Toro* is the Japanese name for tuna belly, which is prized for sushi because it is the fattiest cut.

Wolf-fish: A North Atlantic fish, sometimes referred to as marine catfish, it has fine white flesh which is mild. Wolf-fish is a ferocious cannibal with sharp teeth, hence its name.

Wreckfish: A gray fish related to grouper, wreckfish takes its name from its habit of lurking in wrecked sunken boats. Wreckfish are firm, white, and mild. They tend to grow to be quite large because they can only be caught by line and not with a net.

Japanese Cooking Terms

Agemono: A term referring to something deep-fried, tempura is a form of *agemono* where the food is battered then fried. Some foods, however, are dusted in no more than flour before frying.

Mushimono: A category of steamed dishes (*mushi* means steamed). The most popular example of this is *chawan mushi*, which is basically steamed savory custard.

Nabemono: A category of one-pot dishes cooked at the table: for example, *shabu-shabu*.

Nimono: Simmered dishes—a method of cooking used for fish and meats which call for slow cooking. It also applies to a dish steamed over simmering liquid, for example, octopus that is first rubbed in radish, then steamed over simmering liquid. The resulting octopus is tender with undamaged skin.

Suimono: The Japanese term for clear soups similar to a consommé.

Sunomono: Literally, this means vinegared things and refers to saladlike items that have a vinegar dressing.

Teriyaki: The term refers to a special glaze applied to food in the final stages of grilling or frying. The glaze is generally sweet, based on soy sauce, sake, and mirin.

Tsukemono: Japanese term for pickles like the *umeboshi* plum and a large range of vegetables, similar to the Korean kimchee.

Yakimono: A grilled dish. The grilling may be done over a direct or indirect flame.

Zensai: A term for what we call an appetizer or hors d'oeuvre.

Ingredient Sources

The Internet availability of ingredients that can be difficult if not impossible to find outside large cities in America is nothing short of inspiring. Gone are the days when a cookbook like this would appeal only to New Yorkers and denizens of the Pacific Rim. Now a cook in a cottage in Lakeside, Ohio, can have galangal, pomegranate molasses, Spanish paprika, and even flash-frozen octopus delivered right to her kitchen door.

Here are a few of the best resources:

This umbrella site will link you to every imaginable Asian ingredient resource, by region:

www.asiafood.org/food_linksshopping.cfm

Kalustyan's marvelous resource for those of us in Manhattan, keeps a vast and splendid Web site for cooks outside the city:

www.kalustyans.com

Spanish ingredients, sometimes called for in this book, are all available here:

www.tienda.com

This site is particularly strong on Chinese, Thai, Vietnamese, and Filipino ingredients, but they have many others as well:

www.ethnicgrocer.com/eg/default.asp

Virtually every unusual ingredient in this book will be available at one of these four Web sites.

Index

203

Index